"No Funeral Arrangements"

Memoirs of a Prophet

———————

Eboney Lewis

Book Cover Design by Essential Designs by: Ciara "Ci" Thacker
Professional Pictures by David Wallace at D. Wallz Studios

ISBN-13: 978-0692663851
ISBN-10: 0692663851
Publisher: Anointed Fire House
www.anointedfirehouse.com
Printed in USA by Anointed Fire House

Dedication

I would like to dedicate this book to my mother: "Linda". She was the first prophetic voice I heard, even before I knew what prophetic meant.

To my brother, "Chuck": You are an inspiration to me and I thank you for endowing me with some of your endurance and strength.

To my son, "Shondelle" (A prophetic voice who wasn't born to fit in either): I love you all so very much. Thank you for allowing me to share my journey with you.

To the Ancient of Days: You knew me before I was formed in my mother's womb; it's an honor to be "YOUR" prophetess. To You be all the glory.

Table of Contents

Note from the Author

I wrote this book before I knew I was going to write it. The Lord put these words in my heart long before He instructed me to begin this writing journey. I embarked on a journey from Cleveland, Ohio to Lexington, Kentucky that would eventually set me up for greatness. I needed this book to be written so that I could look back on how my life became what it is today, and in turn, be a blessing to someone in need of a written experience. The words that I wrote were not only used to strengthen my walk with the Lord, but to show others that a calling on your life cannot be undone by the storms of life or the decisions we make, whether they are good or bad. The fact that I am called to be a prophetess *here on earth* clearly showed me that the Lord engrafted the prophetic in me while I was still in my mother's womb (*Jeremiah 1:5*). [*A prophet is one who proclaims or tells a message he has received; a spokesman, a herald, a representative of the Lord. A prophetess is a female prophet*]. I would like to point out that even though this book is about my memoirs, it's also about spiritual growth and allowing the Lord to show you who you really are in Christ. Additionally, this book will show you how the storms of life are used to bring you closer to the Lord. Throughout this book, I want you to ask the Lord to show you who you really are and ask Him what you are called to do in this lifetime.

Introduction

I (Eboney Tatishia Lewis) died on March 28th, 2013, in Lexington Kentucky. There were no funeral arrangements, no obituary column in the newspaper, no witnesses ...NOTHING. I just died. Everything about me ceased to exist on that fateful day. I was already lost in a sense because I didn't think I belonged to anyone. I was wandering in a valley, searching for God and hoping that He would help me find my way. For more than 17 years, I wandered blindly inside a perpetual dark tunnel, a place that would eventually consume me. I was consumed by darkness, sin, anger, hatred, rage, loneliness, and most of all, a thirst that would never be quenched by my own doing.

During my storm, I was not fully aware of God's deep love for me. I doubted that He even loved me at all. Not fully understanding that "HE" wanted me for His own good pleasure. *Ephesians 3:16-19: "That He would grant you, according to the riches of His glory, to be strengthened with might through His spirit in the inner man, that Christ may dwell in your hearts through faith; that you, being rooted and grounded, in love, may be able to comprehend with all the saints what is the width and length and depth and height, to know the love of Christ which passes knowledge; that you may be filled with all the fullness of God."*

I have always wanted to know and understand the greatest mysteries of God. Ever since I was a little girl (about four years old), I would talk to the Lord and ask Him things like: Who are You? Where are You? How was I made? Why does the sun burn me when it's all the way up in the sky? How do I feel the wind when I can't see it? I never knew that God had a prophetic calling on my life even back then as a child, not until He called me out of my comfort zone. I was always inquisitive and questioning everything around me. Even as a little girl, I wanted to know the deepness of everything, and for some strange reason, I knew things, deep things that a child ought not to know. As I got older, I began to search for the Lord even more, and the years I spent wondering why I was unable to make it, why I was unable to cope, unable to win, or most of all, why I was unable to believe I was "somebody" started to change me. Those years were hard for me; most of them were unbearable. My life was a cycle of the same disappointments in different seasons.

My life before I knew I was a prophet was difficult and very harsh, and I didn't fully understand why the Lord would allow me to go through so much turmoil, but I would find the answers to my questions soon enough. This went on for years, and my storms and wilderness experience lasted for almost 18 years. There was a point when I said to myself that my son's 18th birthday was approaching, therefore, he had witnessed me in my wilderness for the entirety of his life. I couldn't imagine going through a purposed storm for almost 20 years, but the truth is that the Israelites didn't think that their wilderness period would last 40 years, but it did. So why should I have thought that I could not go through a "purposed" storm? I had to understand that on March 28th, 2013, the storm that was raging in my life was meant to draw me closer to The Creator, the one who had a purpose for me. *Ephesians 1:11: "In Him also we have obtained an inheritance, being predestined according to the purpose of Him who works all things according to the counsel of His will."*

I was in awe at the very thought that God, the one who is slow to anger and abounding in love, would allow me to go through all types of heartache and pain, ups and downs, highs and lows, joys and sorrows, setbacks, evictions, demotions, depression, rejection, doom and gloom. I thought that the enemy was the only one who did these types of things to God's creation. I was ignorant of how God uses storms to shake up His children and awaken them out of their spiritual slumbers into their true destinies in Christ Jesus. It was amazing to know that even in my low points, the Lord was there, watching over me. He took care of me, even in the midst of my sins and distress. He didn't take His hand off me, and knowing this placed me at His feet in total submission to His will. No one ever told me about how storms work in life. No one ever told me that God would allow all types of things to happen to you in order to "break" you. No one ever told me that I had to die to myself so I could live for Him (*see Romans 6:1-7, Galatians 2:17-21, Ephesians 2:1-10*).

Personal Prayer:

Father, thank You for restoring me and giving me my joy back. Thank You, Lord, for being my life and joy. You have allowed me so many heartaches and setbacks just for me to understand that without them, I would not have called upon Your name. Even though You placed me in perilous situations and the wicked wilderness, I called on You and You rescued me. I thank You, Lord, for never leaving my side. You were always there during my storms and I am forever grateful. My storms ultimately led me straight to You. I don't regret my storms, but rather, thank You for them because they taught me to trust in You and only You. You are the lifter of my head and the song in my heart. I love You forever, Lord. Amen.

Chapter One
Allow Me to Reintroduce Myself

So now I'm dead; my old self that is. I died to sin and my former way of life. At one point, I thought to myself, "What do I need to do to stay dead?" How do I ensure that I won't go back to the way I used to be?" God was preparing me for this time in my life almost 20 years ago. When I think back over my life, on the times that I should have been physically dead or the times when I knew better and still sinned anyway, all I can do is weep and thank the Lord because He spared my life. He definitely had more in store for me than what I was currently allowing. I truly believed that I was the worst of all His creations. I really did some awful things, stupid things, derogatory things, callous things, and wicked things. I could go on and on about how I believe I was the worst of His creations, yet I'm here, telling my story and hoping it can help someone who is going through what I've been through, not realizing that you've been called to greater.

Let's Talk About "Storms"

I want to take the time to talk about my storms in their entirety. This is one of the ways that I can continue to stay "dead" in sin by being completely open to the will of God and totally transparent with you. For the longest time, I thought that God was supposed to work on "my time," but He showed me that He is never in a hurry; it's (His creation) that often demands His timing to be what we feel it should be.

One day, while living in my aunt's basement, I was all by myself and I was worshiping the Lord. I was literally thinking on things of Him and I started to sing in my mind that He was an "on time God." As I was singing, the Lord stopped me and clearly said, "Stop saying that I'm an on time God. That's like saying that I'm almost late. I'm never late or early. I know what is needed and I know the appointed time." After He spoke those words to me, I asked Him, "So, what shall I say then, Lord? What shall I say You are?" "I JUST AM" He replied.

The fact of the matter is, God creates or allows the storms of life to discombobulate, thrash, disembowel, dismantle, and completely break us down to our knees. That may sound somewhat harsh, but there is no other way to put it, especially when it's literally happening in an individual's life. He allows His children to go through storms so they will understand that He alone is in control, and not "us". He creates and allows storms so that we will completely depend on Him for everything, for He is the complete source and sustainer of our lives. God knows exactly what He is doing, and He wants us to accept His will for our lives. (*read Jonah 1:1-17*).

Allow Me to Reintroduce Myself

Matters of the Heart

I was between 20 and 21 years old and the single mother of a beautiful baby boy. I was living in Cleveland, Ohio and my son was and still is my life, so I wanted to be the best mom ever. Being a single parent was one of the hardest challenges I have ever had to face. I had my mom and dad, my son's godmother and my brothers, but the fact of the matter was, my son was my responsibility and I had to raise him with the best of my abilities. I can remember when I was pregnant, I prayed to God to help me because I didn't have a clue as to how to take care of a baby. While I was still pregnant, I decided to dedicate my son back to the Lord since he belonged to Him anyway.

I honestly believe I was led to do this by the Lord and I am thankful that I was obedient to the Holy Spirit. I believe that when I dedicated my son to the Lord, He heard my prayer and He made my son to be a meek, selfless, funny, talented and trustworthy soul. During those early years, searching for God was something I did periodically. I wanted to know more about Him, but I didn't really know how to go about doing that. I was young and extremely inquisitive, so I looked for Him in the only way I knew to search for Him. I attended a church, but I came to a conclusion that I really didn't need the church to find God, plus, I was extremely ashamed of being an unwed, single mother. I felt like I failed in life, somehow. I thought that God wouldn't use me because I was an unwed mother. That's how the enemy crept in and created doubt in my mind. That is how my storms started and how self-hatred began to root itself in my life. I didn't understand how to fight the enemy, especially on a spiritual level. *II Corinthians 10:3-5: "For though we walk in the flesh, we do not war according to the flesh. For the weapons of our warfare are not carnal but mighty in God for pulling down strongholds, casting down arguments and every high thing that exalts itself against the knowledge of God, bringing every thought into captivity to the obedience of Christ."*

I was also dating my son's father at that time and he was not a good person. I won't speak ill of him, even though it was not a healthy relationship. He was selling drugs and leaving my son and me for months at a time. Most of the time, I cried when it came to my son's father. I wanted us to be a family, but he wasn't ready to be a father or a husband. I longed for that type of relationship with him, and this longing followed me into other relationships as well. My relationship with my son's father caused a downward spiral of failure for all other relationships that followed.

The relationships I had were not physically abusive, but they were more of me giving myself away to them wholly, which, in turn, made the men I dated take advantage of me. I can count on my hands the number of men I've dated and each and every one that I dated. I gave myself away to them in mind, body and soul. This pattern of behavior went on for years and I didn't think I would ever be free of wanting someone to love me completely, or love me the way that I loved. This part of my storm happened in seasons. I thought I was happy, and then, all of a sudden, like clockwork, we'd break up. My relationships would hit a serious brick wall, and they would never return to normal. After every failed relationship, I would cry out to God saying, "Lord, why can't I find the love of my life? Why can't I fall in love with the right man?"

I suffered one failed relationship after another; it felt like a never–ending trend. It seemed as though I stayed with a broken heart and that I always stayed in a state of brokenness. It was God's way of telling me that He was and would always be my one true love. *Matthew 22:37-38: Jesus said to him, "You shall love the Lord your God with all your heart, with all your soul, and with all your mind." This is the first and great commandment.*

I hope that this chapter will leave someone thinking about some decisions that were made over their life. Sometimes, we must look into our pasts to better understand why we made the choices we made. I can say that I truly wanted real love, but even through my pain, the Lord showed Himself to me. That's a loving God. *[The amount of brokenness in a prophet's life will determine how they hear from the Lord.]*

Brokenness is a hard pill to swallow, but it's a necessary part of our journey. Don't despise small beginnings because it is in those times that the Lord will eternally intervene, and He will divinely interrupt the very fabric of time on your behalf just to show you real love.

Personal Prayer:

Father, thank You that I am able to come to You with all of my concerns, fears, and prayers. I pray Lord that Your love covers all of my perceived thoughts and doubts. Thank You, Lord, for being everything to me. You are my very existence. I pray that You will use me as You see fit. Please forgive me if I tend to lean on my own understanding. I will forever worship Your glorious name. I pray that I will be a blessing to whomever You allow in my life. You will get the glory and I will receive the benefit for being obedient unto You. I will trust Your will, Father, and I will completely surrender my actions, thoughts, and life to You. I love You, Lord.
In Jesus name I pray. Amen.

Precious Thoughts:

- *Keep a thankful heart.*
- *Let God be the head of your life.*
- *Never settle.*
- *Be transparent so that you may help others in need.*

Allow Me to Reintroduce Myself

- *Be truthful with God.*
- *Pray for structure.*
- *Allow God to work out your issues so you can become a testimony.*
- *Seek to please God instead of man.*
- *Always remember that you are special in God's eyes.*
- *Storms are meant to draw you closer to God.*
- *Love God with all that is within you.*

Chapter Two
It Had to Start Somewhere

I want to make sure that I'm giving some encouragement to someone who might be going through their own storm, not just for newly arisen prophets, but all who are in wildernesses and storms of life. It's good to encourage others as well as yourself. I was still struggling with my love life along with this debilitating need for acceptance. I harbored a tremendous amount of anger and hatred in my heart. This alone was my downfall. I was angry at everything and had a large dose of "I don't care" that fueled my anger. My family and friends can't believe that at one point, I hated myself. I also hated my natural father and my life as a whole; I blamed my father for that. This part of my life is what I was most ashamed of. I was in a very dangerous mode of living and thinking. I became dangerous to myself and it reflected every moment during my storm. It was the beginning of a breakdown.

The Infraction

I was about eight years old when my life came to a crashing reality. My father, the man who was supposed to be my protector, was choosing drugs and alcohol over his family. The things that I saw and did for survival were not good for a little girl to go through. For eight years (between the ages of eight and sixteen), I watched my father destroy himself, his relationship with my mother, and completely annihilate the trust and admiration of his children. This is when my anger began to manifest; it was the root of my hatred. Some of the things I will be disclosing about myself in this book are really hard for me.

I want to be honest, and it hurts thinking back on this life-changing season of my life. I loved and still love my father, but he was really messed up. I can remember the first time I found out he was abusing drugs. It was one of the most horrific visions I had ever seen. What I saw scared me into depression. It was around three o'clock in the morning and my mother made me get up out of a sound sleep to wash dishes. If I would have washed the dishes when my mother told me to wash them earlier that evening, I may not have seen my father doing the unthinkable. We lived in low-income town homes, and in the kitchen, the sink ran parallel to the stove. My dad came in the house and he didn't speak. Instead, he ignored that I was even in the kitchen. While I was washing the dishes, he was making a lot of noise. We had our backs to one another, so I looked over my shoulder and I saw my dad trying to free-base.

I had never seen anyone free-base before, but I knew what he was doing. *Urbandictionary.com defines free-basing as a method of inhaling drugs by holding a flame under a metal spoon filled with cocaine or any crushed pill. One holds a flame under the spoon and collects the fumes from the crushed pills in an empty bottle and the inhales these fumes by taking a hit off the bottle.* Something inside me told me what he was doing and told me what it was called. The thing that scared me the most was the fact that he didn't care that I was right behind him. He was behind his baby girl smoking drugs. I immediately stopped washing the dishes and ran upstairs to my mother, but I didn't make it fully up the stairs before I broke down and started crying. At that very moment, my heart was breaking; it was being shattered into pieces because I knew full well that our family wasn't going to be the same. I didn't know that even then, in that very dark moment, I was flowing in the prophetic.

The knowledge I had and understanding that I felt was overwhelming. It seemed like I could see what was going to happen to the family before my father's drug habit was known to the rest of my family. I saw the end before it began. I eventually got up the stairs to my mother and told her what I had seen. She looked at me and said, "I already know baby." My heart sunk even lower. It was almost instantaneous; my feelings for my father were completely reversed. I was eight years old when that happened to me. After that moment, hatred and low self-esteem became my reality because I believed that I deserved everything that was happening to me.

It Had to Start Somewhere

By the time I was 13 years old, I had already tried to kill myself three times. One time, I slit my wrists, and another time, I tried to hang myself. The last time I attempted suicide, I had taken a lot of pills. In addition to the suicide attempts, I had already had a nervous breakdown. At that time in my life, my dad and I hated each other. I didn't mind telling him how I felt about him either. I would tell my mother what he would do while she was out trying to keep the family afloat by working two jobs. Of course, she would confront him and they would argue and fight, and then he would confront me. My hatred for my father made me stand my ground against him. I wasn't afraid of him at all; I had such a boldness against him. I could be happy and smiling one minute, but when my father was mentioned or if he came around, I would change into a completely different person. I didn't want to be anywhere near my dad. My friends would tell me anytime they saw my father at a neighborhood drug house, and I can't begin to tell you how that made me feel. It wasn't embarrassment that I felt; it was more like rage. So from that point on, life in my home became like a prison. My mother was raising my little brother, and I felt the need to protect him from what my father was doing.

Things got so bad between my father and me that I tried to take his life. I can remember a time when he was drunk and passed out on the living room couch. My mother and brother worked nights, so I was home alone with my dad and little brother. I thought to myself: *I wish he would die.* So

It Had to Start Somewhere

I got a butcher's knife from the kitchen and hovered over him as he slept. I didn't go through with it, but the feeling of wanting to harm my dad continued to grow. My mother eventually had to separate from him, because it became unsafe for my dad to live with us. My oldest brother and I were growing up, and my dad wasn't going to get away with some of the things he'd done when we were children. By the time I was 16 years old, my mother finally had enough. Those years with him there in the house with us, in addition to the years when he was no longer there were years that I needed him in my life. I believe that my father and I both paid the penalty for his absence.

I blamed my father for almost everything that went wrong in my life up until I had my son. Sometimes, people can allow hate to drive them, and that's exactly what I had done. I allowed the hatred of my father to control every area of my life. Could I have raised my son with hatred in my heart? What kind of person would he have turned out to be if I acted out my hatred on a daily basis? I had to cry out to the Lord to help me with the anger and hatred I had towards my father.

It was not an overnight process, but healing did take place. The hatred I harbored started spilling over into other areas of my life. My education suffered, my relationship with my mother suffered, my relationship with my friends suffered, and I was beginning to build walls all around me.

It Had to Start Somewhere

Today, I can safely say that I love my father with all of my heart. We are very close and I can talk to him about anything, but the fact of the matter is, just because I don't hate my father anymore doesn't mean I got rid of the anger that was hidden deep in my heart. I always searched for deeper meanings of my trials and tribulations. I was never settled on being delivered once and that was it. I knew in my core that there was more to it. If we don't confront certain issues that arise in our lives, we can count on them resurfacing at the most inopportune time in our lives.

The enemy knows us by our pasts and by our sinful nature. He will come with the wrongful things you did and try to use those things against you, but we must allow the Lord to deliver us from past hurt. One of the ways to defeat the enemy is to trust in the salvation of the Lord. I know that I'm now free from all hatred. I'm so grateful that the Lord renews the heart because it harbors all types of emotions. Only our Lord and Savior can purify matters of the heart. *Psalm 139:23-24: "Search me, O God, and know my heart; try me and know my anxieties, and see if there is any wicked way in me, and lead me in the way of everlasting."*

This was not an easy chapter to write, but I wrote it to show you the origin of my hatred. When we're transparent, deliverance and healing can start. *[A prophet cannot stray too far from the truth, even if it is at the expense of being transparent about who they are]*. I'm no longer ashamed of my past because I can't control what happened. I want others to see that life happens to us all and if we want to be healed and set free, we must confront the hurt and give it to the Lord. Let the healing process begin and let the "real" you arise.

Personal Prayer:

Father, I need You forever. You are my life. I thank You for being the Living God, full of mercy and grace. Thank You for keeping me in the middle of my mess, sin and distress. Lord, I trust You all the way. I thank You for saving and forgiving me. I am forever grateful for all You have done and will do for me. Thank You for my family, Your perfect will and thank You for Jesus, the one and true Savior. I can't live without Your love for You sustain me. Please Lord, keep me from sinful and deceitful ways, for You did not create me for nonsense, foolishness, nor wicked behavior, but to worship You with my life. I love You. In Jesus name I pray. Amen.

Precious Thoughts:

- Forgive so you can be forgiven.
- Always keep a thankful heart.
- Always see the best in others and yourself.
- Never doubt God's ability to change your situation.
- Always pray and ask God for wisdom and guidance.
- Be completely honest with God.

- Ask God to remove all bitterness from your life, if you don't it will cause a negative chain reaction.
- Never underestimate the power of prayer.

Chapter Three
Let's Face it; I'm a Mess

Like most people, I have a lot of faults. I'm so fragile and small because I'm human, or better yet, I call it being transparent. We all fall short of the glory of the Lord, but yet He calls to us. He calls us to worship His holy name because He is worthy to be praised. He keeps us even in the midst of our iniquities, wrongdoing, set-backs, emotions, and sin. I was still wanting someone to love me, and because of this flaw, my life became a broken revolving door. I was looking for a love that I didn't get from my father and I was determined to not feel empty again.

Some people believe that wanting love makes a person weak, but here's the truth: we are designed for love, and we are designed to love like our Father intended for us to love. Wanting to receive that love in return is an attribute of the Heavenly Father. I found myself in one hopeless relation after another, being dragged down until my spirit was completely bruised and broken. Of course, I don't fault the men I dated because none of them knew the Lord. I fault myself because I gave in and I chose to give them what should have been God's alone. I gave them my entire self.

God said in His Word that He is the only one we should trust, and no one else should get this adoration. *Psalm 118:8-9: "It is better to trust in the Lord than to put confidence in man. It is better to trust in the Lord than to put confidence in princes."* We should never offer adoration to anyone but the Lord for He is the Creator of all things.

[Prophets are known to have their allegiance tested once awakened, and I was not separated from this process. Prophets must align themselves to the Lord in every facet of their lives. This is the main reason I had such a hard time with relationships. My flesh wanted to be satisfied, but my spirit would not compromise]. The Lord will deal with His vessels in such a manner that may seem harsh to others, but it's necessary to be proven fit to be used by the Lord. *Malachi 3:3: "He will sit as a refiner and a purifier of silver; He will purify the sons of Levi, and purge them as gold and silver, that they may offer to the Lord an offering of righteousness."*

A Warped Perception

I had a warped perception when it came to "relational love." What I used to do was look at my friends and other people around me in relationships and I figured that I needed to be on their level. I didn't know if their relationships were working out for them, or if God placed them with each other because it was in His will for their lives. I was looking with my natural eyes, and my own desire for a relational love got the best of me with every relationship I entered.

Everyone wants to be loved; God placed that need in all of His creation. We desire to be loved unconditionally, but what some people fail to realize is that the only one who will completely fill that void of true, unconditional love is Jesus, Himself. He is the only one who loved us first and completely. I truly struggled with this issue all the way up until I realized what my storms meant. I desired to be delivered from this stronghold because I didn't want to mess up any chances of meeting my "real husband." However, I was slowly returning to my old mindset, anytime someone said they liked me, for years, I believed that it meant; "Let's make it last forever!" I saw myself returning to old habits and my old sinful ways, but God tore down that stronghold in my life. It is extremely important that we are delivered from ungodly thinking and it is important for us to stay delivered.

We need to keep a deliverance mindset so that the enemy cannot grab a foothold over us. I praise the Lord for His timing, and I will never again question why He does the things He does. One of the many things I'm thankful for is that He knows what's best for us. *Jeremiah 29:11: "For I know the thoughts that I think toward you, says the LORD, thoughts of peace and not of evil, to give you a future and a hope."* I can honestly say that during these ungodly relationships, I always felt weak. I felt like I was never in control, and in retrospect, I wasn't in control at all.

In 2009, before I asked the Lord to deliver me from fornication, I dated an old high school buddy of mine. We'd dated when we were in high school and we tried to see if we could spark up some old feelings. That was a bad move on my part, and of course, I gave him way too much of me. I thought the relationship was going well and I believed that if I gave him what I thought he wanted, he would love me. I told one of my older aunts about this particular relationship and the first thing she asked me was, "Did you have sex with this man?" I couldn't lie to my aunt; she knew me better than that. I told her the truth; I had slept with him, and she told me something that I still remember and hold dear to my heart to this day. She said to me, "You can't keep giving these men your body. When you do give a man your body, you are attaching yourself to him like you were married."

I Corinthians 6:15-20: "Do you not know that your bodies are members of Christ? Shall I then take the members of Christ and make them members of a harlot? Certainly not! Or do you not know that he who is joined to a harlot is one body with her? For 'the two,' He says, 'shall become one flesh.' But he who is joined to the Lord is one spirit with Him. Flee sexual immorality. Every sin that a man does is outside the body, but he who commits sexual immorality sins against his own body. Or do you not know that your body is the temple of the Holy Spirit who is in you, whom you have from God, and you are not your own? For you were bought at a price; therefore, glorify God in your body and in your spirit, which are God's."

I eventually got caught up in a perversion that was twisted and putrid to the Lord. I began having sex with this man on a webcam. I used to do this in my early twenties when my son was a toddler. I would perform sexual acts in front of an internet audience via the web. I loved the way the crowd loved me. Their attention made me feel wanted in a bizarre and perverse type of way. *[The prophet is hated by the enemy; he loathes the prophetic voices of the Lord. One of the schemes he uses to discredit a prophet is sexual immorality because it defiles from within]*.

Everything about this relationship with this man was disgusting, including the foul smell of our intimacy. The Lord literally severed that relationship because it went against everything He stood for in my life. It was a demonic relationship that was designed to take me from under the will of the Lord. I looked at my aunt and lowered my head in shame. She didn't condemn me, but she did the right thing by using the Bible to rebuke me. I thank God for the wisdom He gave to her because it came straight from the Holy Spirit through her, and it was meant for me to hear it at that very moment. Of course, I didn't take it for the truth right away, but now, I know better.

Let's Face It; I'm a Mess

I trust in the Word of God and I take it extremely seriously, and when He spoke through my aunt to me, He was telling me that He loved me and that my actions were not conducive to a child of God. So now, when I think about all those past relationships, I can see how both sides were so attached, why it was hard to leave and why it hurt so bad when it was over. I was never fully over the men I dated, and when I tried to start a new one, the old relationship came along with me. That's called a "soul tie" but in the worst case scenario. *[A "soul tie", in its simplest form, is two souls tied together in the spirit]*.

Not being delivered of past hurts will always end up maiming a person, but Jesus told me that He would never treat me like that. He said that He would never leave me nor forsake me and I completely believe Him. I desired to be delivered from every ungodly soul tie that meant me harm. All of those relationships that took a toll on my heart, mind and spirit needed to exit my life immediately. This didn't happen overnight; it took some soul-searching and brokenness for me to be delivered.

My desire was for the Lord because I was beginning to realize that I couldn't do anything without Him. I desired for Him to replace all of those damaging soul ties with godly relationships. I renounced every ungodly soul tie that was still attached to me. I repeatedly rebuked them and allowed the Holy Spirit to be released over me. After doing that self-deliverance, I was able to speak of those men and not get angry or depressed if their names were mentioned. I actually love them all and pray for them earnestly.

The Correct Perspective

Now that I fully understand that part of my storm, I was able to overcome it because I knew that God wanted to show me that no one would ever love me unconditionally. Every other form of love comes with conditions because God set it up that way. Understand that you may say that you love your spouse, children, your family, and friends with unconditional love, but that's not entirely true. Furthermore, it's not all bad if you think about it because we're all human.

People fail us all the time, even our loved ones. We get mad when our loved ones let us down, and if you think about it, when they let us down, we get offended, we hold grudges, we ignore them, argue with them, we even stop speaking to them because we harbor ill thoughts on whatever made us mad. What we are demonstrating is love with conditions. That's like saying, "I love you very much, but you can make me very upset with you at times." If someone has ever said "I love you," and then, the word "but" comes after, they are displaying love with conditions. That's putting a condition on love. When someone is angry at a person, it's not a nice thing, and some people may act out their disappointment with shouts and gestures, but is that unconditional love? Is that how Jesus loves us? Not at all.

He is slow to anger and abounding in mercy and love. *Psalm 103:8-9: "The Lord is merciful and gracious, slow to anger and abounding in mercy. He will not always strive with us, nor will He keep His anger forever."*

No one will love us like Jesus loves us. After all, He died for us, and not just one or a few hundred thousand people, but He died for the entire world and He counted it as joy to suffer for you and me. *Hebrews 12:2-3: "Looking unto Jesus, the author and finisher of our faith, who for the joy that was set before him endured the cross, despising its shame, and has sat down at the right hand of the Throne of God. For consider Him who endured such hostility from sinners against Himself, lest you become weary and discouraged in your souls."*

Trust me when I say that every time I think about Christ's finished work on the cross, I have to praise the Lord. Who can say that they would die for someone, let alone die for the entire world, especially when a large part of that world hates you? No one is like Jesus; He is ONE OF A KIND. Therefore, I know that the Lord has my husband in waiting. He is preparing him as well, so I will wait on the Lord's will to be fulfilled. I know that He's getting him prepared for me, as well as getting me prepared for him, but in the meantime, I will continue to run after the heart of the Lord. After He sends my husband to me, we will run after the Lord together. *Psalm 63:1-2: "O God, You are my God; early will I seek*

You; my soul thirsts for You; my flesh longs for You in a dry and thirsty land where there is no water. So I have looked for You in the sanctuary, to see Your power and Your glory."

Personal Prayer:

Lord, I thank You for the "process". While the processing hurts, it is necessary for me to go through in order to walk in favor. I will not compromise my salvation for anyone or anything. You told me that it's not going be like this for long, so I believe everything that You have said. Everything that I've lost, all of the pain, tear soaked pillows, depression, heartaches, all of the setbacks and let downs, all of the faulty relationships, all of the rage, and anger, and all the loneliness and times I thought You weren't there will prove that it was all a set-up. All those low points in my life will prove that You were always in control and You were never in fear of losing me. You knew what it took to bring me to Your feet. So, I thank You for the process; I thank You that You desired me more than I desired You. I thank You that the more I ran from You, the more You chased me. You chased me until I couldn't run any longer and fell into Your loving arms. I don't regret the process Lord; in fact, I praise You for the way You handled me. Divine Interruption! I love You, Lord. Amen.

Precious Thoughts:

- *Seek God's truth always.*
- *Let God shift your perspective.*
- *Bless even your enemies.*
- *God's plans for you are always better than your own plans.*
- *Purity is always the best feature.*
- *Fear is a stronghold...PULL IT DOWN!*
- *Sever all ties with the enemy, for he means you no good thing.*
- *Strive for greatness. Aim to be better than you were yesterday.*

Chapter Four
Old Habits Can Die

It was difficult writing about my relationship with my dad. I don't want to make my father out to be a terrible person. He did those things, and his actions were detrimental to the undoing of our family. Nevertheless, we all have sinned and fallen short of the glory of the Lord. *Romans 3:22-24: "Even the righteousness of God, through faith in Jesus Christ, to all and on all who believe. For there is no difference; for all have sinned and fall short of the glory of God, being justified freely by His grace through the redemption that is in Christ Jesus."*

My father had to be broken like everyone else. He had to go through his wilderness, and he had to realize that he needed God to completely reroute his life. I'm glad to say that he is better than he was before, but the abuse he did to his body has caught up with him. Even so, I feel better about his life now. I can say that I prayed for my daddy each and every day he was out there in the world. I had to ask the Lord to forgive me for praying selfishly because I always lifted my dad up in prayer more than anyone else in my family.

Old Habits Can Die

I no longer say that my father is the reason for all of my issues surrounding anger. I knew that it was up to me to allow God to filter out all of the anger from my heart because I was unable to do it myself. I would get angry over the smallest thing; I never really got upset when things didn't go the way I wanted them to go because I was used to struggling. I would get upset if I felt that I was being disrespected or if I felt that my family was being disrespected. I would get so livid, that I would want to physically fight anyone who didn't recognize or respect me for being "Eboney." There were times when I was in school and got into a heated argument with teachers; I would get irate with them, and eventually get kicked out of the class simply because I felt slighted. Most of my teachers said I was brilliant, but my mouth and my anger issues would be my downfall.

I can't go back in time to change the things I've done, but I can allow the Lord to fix everything that isn't like Him today so I can praise Him with my life like I should. Anger has always led me to sin, just as it's done to a lot of people, and that's why it's so important to be transformed and allow your flesh to die. It's the only way that you will be able to fully understand what it means to be dead in sin and alive in Christ.

Romans 6:1-7: "What shall we say then? Shall we continue in sin that grace may abound? Certainly not! How

28

shall we who died to sin live any longer in it? Or do you not know that as many of us as were baptized into Christ Jesus were baptized into His death? Therefore, we were buried with Him through baptism into death that just as Christ was raised from the dead by the glory of the Father, even so we also should walk in newness of life. For if we have been united together in the likeness of His death certainly we also shall be in the likeness of His resurrection, knowing this, that our old man was crucified with Him, that the body of sin might be done away with, that we should no longer be slaves to sin. For He who has died has been freed from sin."

Fix It Lord

On the miraculous day that I died, it was brought to my attention that I never really allowed my flesh to die. No one explained that part of being a Christian to me. No one told me that dying to sin would prove to be the best thing for my life, and the hardest thing to do as well. The way that anger and hatred were ruling my life had me living in HELL on a regular basis. I was never happy; I thought about all those times that I was angry and hated my life and I actually wanted to scream. I had to go through everything I went through in order to be in a continual state of freedom. Even though the storms that raged against my life were painful remedies, I had to be disciplined by them in order to become righteous in the sight of God. The Lord disciplines His children, and if He doesn't chastise us, we would all be messy and disastrous. We would be spoiled, rotten children.

Old Habits Can Die

Have you ever come across a family whose children were completely out of control? We've all seen children like that, and when we see them, we shake our heads and say something like: "Look at those kids. Their parents ought to be ashamed of themselves for not disciplining them and teaching them to stay in a child's place." Children need discipline, and when children get rebuked, it doesn't feel good; as a matter of fact, it hurts. But the end result of the chastisement is so profound that the child may even start to grow in the righteousness of God. *Hebrews 12:4-11: "You have not yet resisted to bloodshed striving against sin. And you have forgotten the exhortation which speaks to you as sons: My son, do not despise the chastening of the Lord, nor be discouraged when you are rebuked by Him; for whom the Lord loves He chastens, and scourges every son whom He receives. If you endure chastening, God deals with you as with sons; for what son is there whom a father does not chasten? But if you are without chastening, of which all have become partakers, then you are illegitimate and not sons. Furthermore, we have had human fathers who corrected us, and we paid them respect. Shall we not much more readily be in subjection to the Father of spirits and live? For they indeed for a few days chastened us as seemed best to them, but He for our profit, that we may be partakers of His holiness. Now no chastening seems to be joyous for the present, but painful; nevertheless, afterwards it yields the peaceable fruit of righteousness to those who have been trained by it."*

I'm so glad that God loves me enough to make me better. I believe that if we are followers of Christ, we should want to be raised up properly and allow the Lord to get us in alignment with His original intent and purpose for our lives. I've heard some people say that they would rather the world rebuke them than have the Lord rebuke them. I know for a fact that the world doesn't love me; the Lord who created the heavens and the earth loves me forever, and no one can ever separate me from the love of God.

Romans 8:37-39: "Yet in all these things we are more than conquerors through Him who loved us. For I am persuaded that neither life nor death, nor angels nor principalities nor powers, nor things present nor things to come, nor height nor depth, nor any other created thing, shall be able to separate us from the love of God which is in Christ Jesus our Lord." Anytime God decides to align me with His will, He's doing it out of love for me; that's a loving Father.

Personal Prayer:

I want to be able to help others who are going through the same type of storms I went through. It's hard to be unable to move when You want me to move because of past hurts and pains. You keep telling me to STAND, and I sometimes think that I'm going to buckle at the knees, but every day You wake me up with Your Glory and give me the breath of life again. You keep gently telling to me that You will supply all that I need in this lifetime.

I have to continue to trust You with my thoughts, actions, and my very life. I have nothing else to lose at this point. I just don't want to be a loser anymore. I'm tired of failing and falling, crying and stalling, but every time I say something like that, You come back and tell me that I'm not a failure. I will not always lose and I will come out victorious.

Please don't let me forget You Lord as the storms are passing like I have done in the past. Back then, I completely forget where my help came from the minute I'd gotten back on my feet. I don't want to turn my back on You, Lord, especially since You never turned Your back on me. You are always there for me, even when I'm unfaithful to You, when I'm not living a Holy Life, and when I'm in my sin.

I want to always sing of Your goodness; I want to always tell others of how You have never left my side. I want to yell to the world that Your love for me is complete and eternal. There is none like You, Lord. You are God all by Yourself. You lift me up Lord, and You are a mighty standard against all enemies trying to destroy my life. Lord, You are my love; You are my life, even in those times when I've wanted to die. You are the reason that I still live. You have given me a reason to praise Your holy name every day of my existence. I will always pray, talk and share my deepest fears and concerns with You.

I will always speak with You about my feelings and my desires in this life. I will continue to seek out Your will so I can please You with the fruit of my praise. I love You, Lord, and I love to praise You. Your grace is more than enough and You have proven this time and time again. I love You, Lord, and I'm nothing without You. Please forgive me for my weakness, but if I were not weak, I would not call to You. I want to tell You that I need You always and forever.

There will never be a moment when I won't need You, Lord. I need Thee, I want Thee, and I cannot go a moment without Thee. You are my ever present help in times of want, need and in times of plenty. I love You with everything that is in me. Please search my heart, Lord, and change me. Please help me to see myself the way You see me. I want to please You more than anyone in this world.

I thank You for all that You have done for me, all that You are doing for me and all that You will do for me. I know that You will never leave me, and I am so sorry for doubting You. I'm sorry for trusting my eyes and my feelings, instead of trusting You completely. I will continue to stand on Your Word. Father, I will continue to stand on what You've told me. I will continue to search for You and seek You. I will continue to meditate on Your Word. I will continue to praise

You and pray to You. I will continue to trust Your will for my life, and I will continue to love You with all that is within me.

Thank You my Heavenly Father, the one who made me, restores me, the one who is faithful to me. You are the one who is kind, good, and merciful. You are the one who is just and the one who loves eternally. Take me and continue to mold and shape me. Teach me Your ways so that I can help and teach others. I love You, Lord. Amen.

Precious Thoughts:

- *See yourself forgiven.*
- *Know that the Lord loves you completely, flaws and all.*
- *Bring all of your hopes, dreams, desires, thoughts, fears and issues to the Lord for He is more than capable of handling and meeting every need you have.*
- *The blood of Jesus covers a multitude of sins.*
- *Stop condemning yourself.*
- *If you don't like something, pray about it and then speak into the atmosphere the change that you desire, but remember that it must line up with the will of the Lord.*
- *Discipline is needed in order to become a usable vessel of the Lord.*

- *What you've been through or may still be going through can help someone in need. You are a living testimony.*

Chapter Five
The Rejection Files

Rejection is a hard pill to swallow. This is something I had gotten accustomed to throughout my life. I didn't want to admit it, but rejection was the norm in my life and what it did was place inside of me a root of bitterness. I found out later that the Lord used the rejection in my life to draw me closer to Him and to thrust me into a place of transformation, reformation, and restoration. *[A prophet will encounter some form of rejection in his/ her life, and that is allowed by the Lord. This is necessary so that the prophet can overcome fear].*

I faced more than one type of rejection in my life, whether it was from a relationship, career advancement, or even rejection from Christian brothers and sisters. People who look for validation and acceptance from others are often rejected more than others. We tend to place our hearts in the hands of people or things that are irresponsible and incapable of caring for them. I wanted validation and acceptance from my earthly father and my past relationships. When validation and acceptance were not given to me, I was catapulted into a deep depression.

The Lord spoke this word to me to let me know the position He takes as we submit to His authority: *"When you submit to Me, you are no longer responsible for yourself. I am completely responsible for you. I am now your caretaker, way-maker, guide, lawyer, doctor, mother, father, sister, brother, teacher. I BECOME EVERYTHING. To be responsible means to have the job or duty of dealing with and taking care of something or someone. I am more than able to be trusted to do what is right and to do the things that are required to keep you."* It is comforting to know that in the midst of it all, God is totally responsible for His vessels, and He knows the plans that He has for us.

A Glutton for Punishment

It seemed that I chased after fulfillment in all the wrong places. I was a bona fide people-pleaser who always got the short end of the stick. I blamed myself entirely because I gave my all when all I had to do was be myself. Sometimes, we assume that people desire us to lay down to get walked over, but instead, we insert that mentality ourselves and it causes us to submit to an inferiority complex that we will have to eventually be delivered from. When we submit to an inferiority complex and are rejected by someone, we tend to own the rejection and we then allow it to become a part of a systematic type of living and thinking.

Even though I was bound by this way of thinking, the Lord eventually renewed my mind and turned it into one of serving. I have always served, even when I was a child. I've never had an issue with serving, so people-pleasing became second nature to me. I over-compensated on my past jobs. I tried to let my employers know that I was the woman who would break the mold, and go above and beyond to be the employee of the year. I pressured myself all the time to be the best so I would never get looked over.

I stayed in seclusion because I feared being rejected, especially by the people who signed my paychecks. So when I wasn't the best or if I slacked, I would act out on the job. Calling off, not feeling like doing my work, having the wrong attitude about my job, speaking ill about my job and co-workers, just acting out how I was feeling about not getting recognition or love from the workplace. I behaved like this on every single job I had.

I would never work at one place for a long time. The lengthiest employment I had was three years. If I didn't quit my job, I would get fired. This was like a revolving door, over and over and over again with places of employment. It resembled how I was with my relationships. When one job didn't work out, I would pray to God for a new one. My feelings toward this type of rejection were bitterness and fear. Rejection was the root of all of my fears and I didn't recognize it. I feared that if I couldn't keep a job, then I would become a bad mother to my son because I couldn't provide for him. I feared losing my car because I couldn't keep up with the payments, no food in the house, no security, no safety, just living in total fear.

Living in fear is not normal behavior. I would go off into daydreams and picture myself homeless and leaving my son with my mother to end my life because I felt he was better off with her. The fear that gripped me was severe, all because I felt rejected by life in general. Fear and bitterness were the driving forces in my life at this point, which drove me to make very rash choices. I believed wholeheartedly that my life was never going to get better due to so much rejection. I was miserable and my misery wreaked havoc on my life. I learned how to settle into those harmful feelings. With these two evil spirits controlling me, it was hard for me to think clearly. I was a believer in Jesus Christ, but I had the wrong mindset. I was a double-minded Christian. *James 1:5-8: "If any of you lacks wisdom, let him ask of God who gives to all liberally and without reproach, and it will be given to him. But let him ask in faith with no doubting, for he who doubts is like a wave of the sea driven and tossed by the wind. For let not that man suppose that he will receive anything from the Lord; he is a double-minded man, unstable in all his ways."*

When I was employed, I believed that I was in a place of stability, but when I lost my job, I lost all hope. I believed God for one season and lost faith in Him in the next season. How was it that I allowed my thinking to be completely mangled and twisted? Why did I allow my mind to hold on so tightly to these feelings? A double-minded person is drawn in two opposite directions. The Lord tells us to be transformed by the renewing of our minds, but He also tells us that our whole lives need to be given as living sacrifices for this is acceptable to the Lord. If our lives are not lived for the Lord in their entirety, then all hell will break loose in our minds and lives. *Romans 12:1-2: "I beseech you therefore, brethren, by the mercies of God, that you present your bodies a living sacrifice, holy and acceptable to God, which is your reasonable service. And do not be conformed to this world, but be transformed by the renewing of your mind, that you may prove what is that good and acceptable and perfect will of God."*

My negative feelings caused a major shift in my life. My feelings were constantly hurt and rejection became a way of life for me. We have to conquer rejection because it's so common in everyday living; there's no way around it. In some form or fashion, rejection will be seen by the human eyes and felt by someone every day.

Being delivered from rejection didn't come easy because I continued to face it on a daily basis. The one thing that the Lord taught me about it was to not allow it to enter my mind because it can cause irreversible damage. Rejection can be taken two ways: either we can let it ruin our perspective on life or we can thank God for it because it can save us from a world of misery.

Personal Poem:

Honestly...
You're kidding me, right? Is there any other reason? Honestly, I don't know. It's not dead for now, but if we don't fix it, surely there's no way to get it back. Yes or No? Look at where we've come from; we're to blame for our own destruction, our own warped sense of thinking, and our own demise.

But I want to live free in truth, in light, in love, but honestly, I'm scared of you, and you, and that one over there. Is there any other way to break free of this? To be afraid is unhealthy. It allows you to become complacent with life and your surroundings. Never let your situations dictate what you will become.

Honestly, I'm tired of all this, so I'm running and I'm winning now. I've run this race too many times to not know what the outcome is. I saw a couple potholes, so I jumped over them. And yes, I stumbled, but I didn't fall. Honestly, I've never believed what they said. I keep my head pointed up to the sky, that's my help, truth, faithfulness, and love. Was that it? I mean... really; it can't be that simple, but as I look around, I see some catching up to me. It's about time, but remember, time waits NOT.

You all better catch up; some new things are going on and I have on my running shoes for this one. Honestly, looking back, I was afraid of you, you, and you over there, but now that I think of it, I was only afraid of myself. I've shaken it off now and it's gone, so let's go, come on; we have to fix it, whatever it takes. It's brand new; no old stuff. Honestly, fixing it was the best thing that ever happened to me.

Precious Thoughts:

- *No matter what you do, your steps are ordered by God.*
- *God will always restore what was lost to you; believe He will do it.*
- *Fear is never an option. Refuse to worry about anything.*
- *Cast your cares on God; He can handle everything.*
- *Thank God in all things.*
- *Do not let the fear of rejection drive you away from the salvation of the Lord.*
- *Renounce every bit of evil the enemy sends your way, and remember, deliverance is ongoing.*
- *For God has not given us the spirit of fear, but of power, love, and a sound mind. – II Timothy 1:7*

Chapter Six
Uncomfortable Zones

So much happened in the year of 2011 that I had to sit back and replay it all to put it in chronological order. I found myself asking the age old question, "Why is this happening to me?" I was going through one of the harshest times ever in my life and nothing could have prepared me for what I was about to encounter. If someone would have told me that I was going to face life, death, and maybe an uncertain outcome, I wouldn't have believed them.

Injury, job loss, setbacks, sickness, eviction, education letdown, and loneliness were some of the issues that I figured I had to accept as "my life." It was like I became content or comfortable with the hand I was dealt. I tried to tell myself that my life, at that point, was normal and that I was spiritually and mentally capable of handling all that bombarded me in a matter of months. I didn't take into account that my life was a revolving door of error, and because I'd been down that road before, I knew the end result would be catastrophic. At this point, I didn't want any more comfortable situations. I didn't want any more issues that took years for me to overcome. I desired peace, but I often wondered if I'd ever find it. *[A Prophet will be tried and tested by fire. This is God's way of exposing the prophet to the harshness of a life not in His will. This is necessary because the prophet will need to solely depend on the Lord for everything, for He is their source and He provides their resources.]*

This is Only a Test

In life, we, as believers, are put through many tests by the Lord to see what is in our hearts. The Lord surely led the Israelites through the wilderness to test their hearts and see if they would keep His commandments. They failed countless times, but the Lord saved them countless times as well. *Deuteronomy 8:2: "And you shall remember that the Lord your God led you in the wilderness, to humble you and test you, to know what was in your heart, whether you would keep His commandments or not."*

The most important aspect of this test is remembering that God will lead and keep you, which is something I carelessly forgot. Even when we forsake the Lord, He's still in the midst of our situations, hardships, and chaos. This holds true when my older brother had a stroke on January 15th, 2011, just seven days before his 38th birthday. I will never forget that terrible, yet awesome day. God was in the midst of us, and He led the way the entire time. I didn't see it, but God orchestrated the entire scene. It was like an Oscar-worthy film and God was the executive producer and director.

It all happened on a Saturday morning. I heard a loud knock on my door. I was fast asleep on my living room couch, so the loud knocking really startled me. I looked through the peephole and saw my little sister. I knew something was wrong because she was out of breath when I finally opened the door. She could barely get the words out of her mouth. She yelled, "Something is the matter with Chuck and Momma is on the floor crying and screaming!" I tried to wake up by wiping my eyes so that I could clearly see her face; she was terrified. "What's wrong?" I asked. What she said to me didn't make any sense. My sister told me that something happened to Chuck and that he was in the hospital. I shook my head in disbelief because I figured that he had gotten into an argument with his girlfriend at the time. I thought to myself, "She better not have harmed my brother." What could have happened that my brother was sent to the hospital?

I calmed my sister down and told her to head back to Mom's house. My mother and I lived in the same apartment building in Euclid, Ohio. I stayed in building B and my mother and sister stayed in building A; that's why my sister was able to get to me so fast. I hurried up and threw some decent clothes on, woke up my son and told him to put on some clothes as well. I told him that I was headed to his grandmother's house to see what was going on with his uncle. As I was walking across the parking lot of the apartment complex, I got a bad feeling about what I was about to see.

When I walked into my mom's house, I saw that she was standing in the middle of her living-room and the color was completely gone from her face. My mother has a mocha skin complexion, so for her color to be non-existent, I knew it was bad. "What's the matter; what happened to my bother?" I asked. She walked up to me slowly and looked up at me and said words that still bring me to tears. She said, "Your brother is bleeding in his head." I couldn't explain the condition of my heart when my mother said those words. I can only remember that I was looking up at the ceiling and screaming at the top of my lungs, and when I started screaming, my mother started screaming too. I only stopped when my mother shook me and told me not to freak out. Her words were, "Eboney, please. I need you to stay calm. If you freak out, then I'll freak out. I need you." What my mother said stuck with me the entire weekend. I got myself together and took her to Cleveland Clinic, where my brother was hospitalized.

I made sure that my son was aware of what was happening, but I made him stay behind because he was very close to his uncle. I knew that if he went with me to the hospital that I would have too much on my hands. By the time my mother and I got to Cleveland Clinic, we were told that my brother was in route; he was delayed. My mother and I were still wondering how Chuck fell in the first place.

While he was in route to Cleveland Clinic, we were told by his then girlfriend what really happened to him. My brother had decided to go into work that Saturday morning to put in some overtime. Prior to the weekend, he said that he was feeling a headache coming on, but headaches were something that he got accustomed to, so he shrugged it off. He left home to go to work with a full blown migraine, which he later described to us as a headache of epic proportions. He said that it was the worst he'd ever had, but he pushed himself to go to work.

Then what he explained to us next, we believed was supernatural. He said that the pain got so unbearable that he blacked out while he was driving, and there was a time that he didn't remember because he blacked out. He decided to turn around and go back home, but he blacked out by the time he tried to turn the car around to head back home. Chuck said that he remembered driving behind an 18 wheeler truck, but the next thing he remembers was that he was in the driveway of his home.

He stammered back in the house and heard the voice of his girlfriend. She asked him what he was doing back home, and he told her that his head was in so much pain that he couldn't make it to work. He then tried to lie down and sleep it off, but his girlfriend said he started gritting and biting down on his teeth because of the searing pain. His girlfriend was a nurse practitioner in training, so she knew that something was terribly wrong with him; she knew that she had to get him to the emergency room and fast. Since Chuck lived in another county, it would have taken at least 30 minutes to get him to the Cleveland Clinic, so he was taken to a hospital emergency room where he actually resided instead in Painsville, Ohio.

The ride to the hospital in Lake County was touch and go. He was in and out of consciousness and his girlfriend stated that he was moaning and groaning in pain. Of course, she was afraid because Chuck's condition was becoming more crucial by the second. At the emergency room, as he was getting admitted, Chuck said that the pain in his head had become unbearable. He was trying to sit patiently, but in an attempt to get seen right away, he stood up and asked what was taking them so long. He tried to explain to them that he was in a lot of pain, and right then, he collapsed.

They eventually got him on a gurney and took him straight to the back to be seen because his condition was critical. His girlfriend was told that it didn't look like he would survive, so they advised her to call his family to tell them the bad news. She couldn't find it in her heart to call my mother with the bad news, so she demanded that the hospital life flight him to the Cleveland Clinic. We waited at the Cleveland Clinic, supported by some other family members. Most of my extended family were there. We were all hopeful, but we kept looking at my mother to make sure she wouldn't lose it or break down.

I thank God for my mother; she constantly prayed for my brother during this catastrophic test. She stayed in constant communication with the Lord. My mom said that while we were still back home getting prepared to check on my brother, she prayed to the Lord. She said to Him, "Father God, whatever you decide is best for Chuck, so be it. If you let him stay, You're good, and if You decide to take him, You're still good." She demonstrated to me that trusting God, even in the midst of uncertainty, even when it may turn out for the worst doesn't negate the fact that God is good and that He is in complete control. I would later learn how to tap into and release that kind of faith and trust God over my life.

So much happened within the span of the weekend that my brother had a stroke. Miraculous strength, healings, tears, deliverance, and lives changed all happened in those two days. As a family, we prayed, cried, prayed some more, anointed the hands of the doctors attending to my brother with oil, and even watched a woman on her death bed be healed completely by the Holy Spirit. I saw God work in such a way that forever changed the way I perceived Him. I knew that I had to take the restrictions off of God and allow Him to take me on a faith ride.

That Saturday morning, my brother had emergency surgery to find and repair the tiny vessel that was bleeding in his head. The surgery was successful, but I was still afraid. Even though the surgery was successful and he was on the road to recovery, the next 48 hours of his life were crucial. There was nothing any of us could do at that point. We knew that we all needed to continue to pray and believe that he was completely healed. My family had to force me to leave for some rest. I didn't want to leave my brother for a moment. I wanted him to know that I was there and that I loved him, but I gave in to weariness.

As I entered my apartment, I made sure that my son was tucked in bed, and I found myself resisting sleep. Every time I closed my eyes, I saw my brother and wept. As I cried, I could softly hear the Lord speak to me. He spoke a mighty word that settled my weary spirit and allowed rest to be my portion. The Lord said to me, "He is strong; he is strong. I made him strong. I made Chuck strong for such a time as this." I began to speak the word He spoke to me, and I drifted off into a peaceful sleep. My brother was in the hospital from January to April of 2011. It was a long road, but God healed him, and he is alive and living with me today.

The rest of 2011 was extremely tumultuous. Things were falling apart. My mother's back injury from 2009 was not getting any better. I still couldn't find work. I felt like I had been blackballed. I had to fight to get unemployment from my past employer, and by the time I was able to get it, I was behind on all my bills. I was fighting my way through nursing school, trying to make good grades in all my classes. Every day, my heart was breaking. I cried but kept most of the tears from my family. I would take care of my brother after I got out of school, and then, my mom would go off to work. I would do my best to aid my mother and brother, and at the end of the day, I would go to my apartment and cry out to God.

Some nights, I would often cry myself to sleep, I would just spend time in silence thinking about where my life was heading. And then, there were some nights that I would hear the voice of the Lord calling to me. I would hear Him speak to my spirit, "Come away with me, beloved." I would then spend all night and morning with Him, just worshiping Him, and allowing Him to soothe my brokenness. *Psalm 34:17-19: "The righteous cry out, and the Lord hears, and delivers them out of their troubles. The Lord is near to those who have a broken heart, and save such as have a contrite spirit. Many are the afflictions of the righteous, but the Lord delivers him out of them all."*

Eventually, I had no choice but to be taken out of my comfort zone. My family in Cleveland was definitely a cushion. Those needing me the most almost kept me from hearkening to the command of the Lord. A third eviction notice was the breaking point. I made the decision to step out in faith and go off into the unknown. I broke my family's heart when I told them that I had no other choice but to leave and try and make it far from them. My mother's face hurt me, my son's anguish was evident in his body language, and my oldest brother's voice shuttered with fear as departure was before us. Leaving the known to go into the unknown was something that the Lord permitted. My life would be forever changed when my son and I embarked on a journey to answer God's mighty call on our lives.

Personal Prayer:

Father, there is no one like You anywhere. I have searched to no avail. You are everything to me. Never has anyone ever took me and shaped me, cared for me, redeemed me, restored me, protected me, and loved me like You have. There is none like You, Lord. You are, by far, my only one true love. You are, by far, my heart's desire. You are, by far, my best friend. You are my beating heart, the air that I breathe, and my very reason for living. I carry You in my heart, my mind, and my spirit. I need You forever. Amen.

Precious Thoughts:

- *Never doubt that God can fix the bad circumstances in your life.*
- *God is and has always been the true source.*
- *Press your way through the pain.*
- *Take time out to be still and meditate on the things of God.*
- *When God moves, make sure you have a one-way ticket that cannot be revoked.*
- *Seek rest, for it is needed.*
- *Seek alone time with the God often.*

- *Never stop believing that the Lord will work everything out.*
- *Share God's love and compassion for you with others.*

Chapter Seven
This Basement

This basement; cold, hard, dark, deep basement. You placed me here in this basement. You placed me here to reveal my true testament. While lying on the cement, You pushed me, tested me, broke me, and then, let me face this basement.

I wasn't ready; I wasn't steady. I wasn't right and I put up a fight, but You won. This basement has now become my prison. Not here, in this basement, not here, but I was sent, not of my will but Yours became the movement, this basement. Banished I thought, that it was all my fault, my punishment not so affectionate, why have I been downcast and sent to this basement?

This basement is my hell; this basement is my prison, this is not a heavenly mission, this is a BASEMENT! My home away from home, where I've become desolate and alone. A peculiar person there must be a syndrome, I'm unable to answer the conundrum of this basement. Dazed and confused on why this basement has been used. This basement is the backdrop of a methodically intricate plot, one I might add, I did not volunteer or opt. But I'm here in this basement, in prison already serving time spent, not

This Basement

understanding my placement, but God revealed the true sacrament, the meaning of this basement.

But its meaning I care not to know. It's a hard place, full of disgrace, bitterness, and a love that's misplaced. How can You show the meaning of this empty hole, this basement where my brokenness dare to unfold, where eternity and time meet and explode?

The chastisement of my flesh, You placed me in this basement to arrest. You've placed me in shackles until Your proper authority was faced; until this purposeful storm that was raging was fully embraced.

I'm looking for answers for this basement placement. My tears became the trails of detachment. Sorrowful weeps and pools of tears on the concrete, beating my chest, I am but a blemish, a speck, but in spite of me, You saw my need and it was forever met.

Confusion, spinning in the deep places of my heart. I can't hear You in this basement, the light is just too dark. You whisper sometimes telling me that You are near, whispers in my mind but all I feel is fear. I begin to search for You in this basement, but I want so bad to let go, I'm dying naked on the pavement. I'm folding, even caving in, but I'm still here in this basement.

This Basement

I begin to look around; my physical body is being torn down, broken into nothing, but this basement is the start of something. It's starting to reveal the real meaning of submission and why I 'm nothing but a limited edition.

I cry aloud, "LORD, WHY AM I HERE?" You tell me… I sent you first. First to this basement, nothing you have been through will be wasted. I have never left you, nor forsaken. Child, you are Mine, and the plans I have for you are truly divine. You are the branch, and I'm the true vine. Your brokenness I did require, because I have much for you to do, and you were living a life uninspired. I desire for you to live and show the brokenhearted what I did. Tell them how I took you from death to life, and now, you live for Me without guilt or strife.

I want you to abide in Me, to go out and glorify Me. I will make you a blessing, and make your cause as clear as the bluest seas. I created you separately; trust in me and you will see all that I have in store for you. My word you can stand and know it to be true. Remember when you asked Me child, when will it be your turn? I call you forth now to be my soldier, in service you will not return, the way you once were, dead in your flesh; for I am your teacher, and the teacher is always quiet during the test.

I knew what it took to bring you to your knees. To call on the Living God, as hard as it seemed. I want you to know that this in fact was intentional. I called you forth from eternity on, your life has been ordained, and no mistakes have I made. You are now Mine, as always child; I have captured your life and am restoring it in my own time. I desire your allegiance, worship only Me, remember I said to you, Praise Me, for I will in turn bless thee. Seek Me still, in the dark of night, seek Me even still, while the sunlight still gleams bright. Seek Me when all else fails, seek Me child because My Love will ALWAYS PREVAIL!

I want to show you your worth, how much I truly love you; nothing you will ever do now will haunt you. I will cleanse you whole, make your light shine completely through your soul, and allow all to see, the beautiful and perfected masterpiece. You see, I knew all along that you were a vessel, someone who would keep my Laws, My princess who is extremely special.

You are needed in the kingdom of light, your plight is what caused you to fight; you are a beautiful solider, a fighter for Christ, now rise up and get equipped with My Spirit that will suffice. I will teach you My Word and show you My will, My favor is upon you, but you have to be still. Listen to My voice and follow My direction, because what will follow then is My complete and utter blessings.

I will place you in the middle of things, when My people need to hear from Me, I will send you forth to preach fervently. Do not be afraid, because it was you that I made, courageous and strong, loud and able to suffer long. I moved throughout your life, placing you under harsh conditions, for such a time as this, and now you're like a loaded gun with My Word as your ammunition. I know you have wondered if I really loved you; as you can see now, I place no one above you. My child, I see My son's precious blood all over you, it saturates and engulfs you through and through.

I'm starting to see; I can feel the stirring. This is a process and it's not to be hurried. My tears have been washed, my face has been cleared, the oil is being poured and has since then been smeared. The anointing is heavy, my life is now bold, His power is completely embedded within me and to Him I'm completely SOLD, and so....my life is not my own.

The Cave of Adullam

I instinctively started this chapter off with a poem that the Holy Spirit authored called, "This Basement." I began to write this while in what I would call a "basement" or "cave." By this time, I was so broken and shattered, not fully understanding that in this state, God had me right where He wanted me. He wanted to start with a blank canvas. The Cave of Adullam is the cave spoken of in the Bible where David went to hide from Saul. This is the cave where God started preparing him to become King. There, in that cave,

David was stripped of himself and rewired. He was being prepared to become King so this cave had a purpose.

[*Preparation always comes before purpose and transformation always comes before duty. This is so significant for the prophet. When he or she is called, there is a "pruning" or "preparation" that takes place. After that, there is a "training season", and lastly, there is a "sending forth" of the prophet. Every true prophet of God will go through this development*]. The call of my prophetic office training started when I moved from Cleveland, Ohio to Lexington, Kentucky with my son. Everything seemed to be going perfectly wrong in my life. One tragic thing after another was happening to me, and it seemed as if it was happening like clockwork. During my brother's recovery, I lost my job. I was working for a major dental corporation in Cleveland while going to nursing school. To make matters worse, I failed the nursing entry exam twice, so I was hurt and dejected on a grand scale. I was living on my own with my son, with no one to help me.

I was overwhelmed by my bills and I was definitely in over my head. I had to fight to get unemployment benefits, and when I was finally approved for it, I was still unable to catch up with the bills because I was too behind on them. Fear was beginning to rear its ugly head again, and it was manifesting faster than it had in the past. My son wasn't producing the best grades in school, plus, my mom had injured her back on her job. She wasn't doing so well trying to work and take care of my older brother. I gained so much weight that I began to have severe back spasms; the list just goes on.

When I moved to Lexington, my life didn't change right away like I thought it would. The challenges I faced were even more overwhelming than before. Terrible dead-end jobs, family hating my son and me, my body began breaking down from fatigue and neglect, and God's voice was completely muted in my life. I was reluctant when I asked one of my mother's youngest sisters if my son and I could move down to her home in Lexington, Kentucky.

My aunt and her family had always been so gracious to other people by letting them live in their home while they tried to establish themselves in Kentucky. I had no other choice because I had been served eviction papers from the apartment I lived in. I could no longer live in a place I couldn't afford. I was spinning out of control and was getting so dizzy because I didn't understand why I had the feeling of having to pick up and leave the entire state of Ohio. I didn't want to leave my mother or my brother, but I didn't get what I wanted. *Proverbs 19:21: "There are many plans in a man's heart, nevertheless the Lord's counsel; that will stand."*

I just knew right away that after I moved to Kentucky, I was going to get a job, get on my feet, and start anew with my son. I thought life was going to get better fast, but I was wrong. When God tells you to do something, most of the time, it's not logical. [*God places His prophets in odd opportunities, perplexing pitfalls, crazy catastrophes, and straight-jacket situations. God doesn't make sense to the world, and at one point, He wasn't making any sense to me either*].

My son and I finally moved to Lexington, Kentucky on August 3rd, 2012. We both had mixed feelings about moving. My son was not on board at first, but he came around when he saw that we were on the road and not turning back. As for me, it took me more time to accept the fact that I wasn't in Cleveland anymore. Not being able to see my mother's face put me in a state of denial for the first couple months.

As soon as I got settled, I found a customer service job and enrolled my son in high school. I was off and running. I hadn't been able to find a job back home in Cleveland for over a year, so to be working and bringing in some income made me feel like I was a part of society again. Within one month, I had moved out of the state of Ohio to Kentucky, gotten my son enrolled in high school and landed a job. I was beaming with joy. It had never dawned on me that I had to live in a basement, and not just figuratively, but literally. My family had an extra room that they allowed my son to sleep in, but I had to take the basement because I had no other place to sleep. In this basement, I had to face facts and realize that I needed God...not just for some things, but for all things. In the basement, I was stripped of selfish desires, abandoned and left alone by reason. I was broken and wounded by my own transgressions, and I was emptied of self-preservation. The basement was the chastisement of my flesh and consecration all in one.

It's About Time

In December of 2012, my job turned into one of the worst jobs I'd ever had. I had never considered that the company I was working for had such a high turnover rate with customer service agents. I had tunnel vision when I moved to Kentucky, and I wanted to get on my feet so bad that I never took the time out to talk with the Lord to learn what my "real" next move should have been. I was suffering a great deal, and I ended up getting extremely sick on New Year's Day. I caught the flu that was going around on the job. I ended up with a double ear infection, upper respiratory infection, and strep throat. I was in pretty bad shape, and as I was trying my best to go into that horrid place, I heard the Lord tell me to not go back to my job. He told me to quit. The Lord was commanding me to do something that didn't make any sense to my mind, but I was compelled to obey. I was starting to drift back into an uncertain future yet again, but this time, I heard the Lord speak loud and clearly about a direction that contradicted all logic from a worldly viewpoint. After I was free and clear of all distractions, I was left all alone. God placed me in an extreme wilderness and in enemy territory.

Darkness started to take me and I was left alone with my thoughts day and night. I tried looking for work, but jobs eluded me, just like back home in Cleveland. I wept every day and most of the time, I cried myself to sleep. My pillows were soaked with tears. I could feel the hurtful words surrounding me from my family members. I had an odd feeling that I was being talked about, belittled, scorned and cursed. I knew that they were also speaking reproachfully about my son. We were the talk of the family and I felt their damaging words in the core of my being. I knew exactly what was being said about my son and me, but there was nothing I could do about it. If they only knew how I felt, then maybe the words wouldn't have been so damaging. My family didn't understand that the Lord told me to quit my job. When a person comes from a worldly family, and they really don't know Jesus personally, they tend to speak and think from a carnal mind, and they cannot perceive things of the spirit.

John 14:17: "The Spirit of truth, whom the world cannot receive because it neither sees Him nor knows Him; but you know Him, for He dwells with you and will be in you." [*Being a prophet is no easy task. The Lord often breaks a prophet by allowing hurt, pain, and rejection (among other things) to bring the prophet to a point of submission*].

Day in and day out, I was being brought even lower than I was the day before. I was confused as to why I was even in Kentucky. My outward appearance was starting to show my vulnerability. I had no defense; all the strength that

I thought I had was diminishing. I questioned my identity, which led me to question God. I would lie in the darkness of the basement crying uncontrollably. I wasn't hearing the voice of the Lord and it became like dead silence. Only my groanings and wailings were heard. I got to the point where I started getting angry; I started demanding answers from the Lord.

I remember the night that started a roaring fire; it only took a spark. There was such a stillness in the basement; it was very quiet, and the only light source was from a night light in the far off corner. I definitely wanted to talk to the Lord because I was tired of crying and not hearing or feeling Him near me. So I began questioning Him, asking Him the questions I felt needed to be answered.

With tears in my eyes, I asked Him, "Why did You send me down here to a basement, Lord? I could have stayed in Cleveland and slept on my mom's floor! You said that You would never leave me; well, You're not here with me. I'm all alone! Why did You leave me?" It didn't take the Lord long to respond. He was waiting on me to say how I really felt, to let out all of my frustrations, fears, and anger. This showed me that He loved me and that He never left me.

His answer was priceless. He simply said, "Finally! It's about time you said something." I just laid on my bed in total silence for what seemed like hours. I was paralyzed because

This Basement

I was surprised at His response. I thought to myself, "What I said wasn't nice at all, and yet You answered me Lord?" I felt in my spirit that He was waiting for me to release all my cares upon Him because He cared (and still cares) so deeply for me.

I Peter 5: 6-7: "Therefore humble yourselves under the mighty hand of God that he may exalt you in due time, casting your care upon Him, for He cares for you." I began to wipe the tears away from my eyes. I sat up on my bed and just basked in His presence. It was an awesome feeling to know that He was there and that He literally heard my cry *Psalm 18:6: "In my distress I called upon the Lord, and cried out to my God; He heard my voice from His temple, and my cry came before Him, even to His ears."*

This was the beginning of some very harsh times while in the basement. The Lord spoke to me quite frequently after that time that I finally cried out to Him. There were times I wanted to give up, especially when I had been stripped of what I thought I needed to survive in this world. Even still, I began to really search for the deeper things of God. I began to chase after Him with a passion that was unbridled. I still cried every day because I didn't fully understand why I was where I was, nevertheless, I kept pressing. I wanted to fully understand that season in my life and in my son's life. I wanted to know why it felt like I was the only one going through this type of shifting. He was getting me prepared for the call on my life. I can't say that I was all for it, but denying God was not a part of the plan.

Personal Prayer:

Father, please continue to guide me. I need You at all times; my heart depends on You Lord. You are taking me from glory to glory, and in this transition, please keep me humble. Please keep me before You, Lord. Please continue to help me remain completely obedient to Your will. I cannot do anything without You. You are my guide, my help, my shield, my truth, my song, and my love... forever. I will praise You for all eternity because You have caused my heart to thirst for You. Father, I will not compromise my salvation for anyone or anything. You are my true foundation. As You send me off into a destined life, please surround me with Your grace, mercy, favor, righteousness, kindness, and most of all, Your love. Holy Spirit, please continue to guide me to the preordained steps mapped out for me through Christ Jesus. Amen.

Precious Thoughts:

- *Just because you follow Jesus Christ doesn't mean you will not encounter trials in your life.*
- *Always be willing and ready to obey God.*
- *Stop talking and listen to what the Lord is saying.*
- *The Lord hears your cries and sees your tears.*

This Basement

- *Even at your lowest, God is still with you.*
- *Just because you don't hear or feel the Lord doesn't mean He's not there.*
- *God knows the plans that He has for you. Let Him show you what they are.*
- *The shifting won't always be painful.*

Chapter Eight
You Want Me To Do What Lord?

A prophet called to God's people sounds like a big responsibility. When I think about being called as a prophet, I really didn't know what to feel or even how to feel. I was thinking to myself: *Who in their sane mind wants to be a prophet?* From what I could decipher, prophets were hated, but not by the world as much, but prophets were hated by "church folk." Many saints in the church have such a misguided view regarding prophets, especially if the saints are not prophetic themselves or they were brought up in churches that didn't believe that prophets still exist today.

[*The prophetic is the ministry work of the prophet and the disciplines and practices of revelatory ministry-The Prophet's Dictionary by Dr. Paula Price*].

Since I haven't been to every church in this world, I can't judge every person in the body of Christ on their views of God's prophetic office. I can only say that I didn't know too much about the prophetic until God called me. I believed in prophets and the rest of the five-fold ministry because I attended a church that operated in the full gospel, or better yet, the full scope of God's order when I lived in Cleveland. I could at least identify what a prophet was, or so I thought. It took me some time to really settle into my new identity. I tried my best to reject the office of the Prophet.

I remember the day that God actually called me. I was in Lexington at my family's home where my son and I were temporarily living. It was a beautiful afternoon in March of 2013. I was home alone and everyone was either working or in school. I was jobless, alone, scared, feeling like a failure to God and my son, and I was doing what I always did while at my family's home: crying. I was in the kitchen trying to prepare something to eat for myself, but I couldn't get myself together to even fix a simple sandwich. I was allowing my feelings to overtake me, and then, out of nowhere, I heard God's still, small voice say to me, "In order for you to speak about Me, you must know Me."

I stopped making the sandwich and started to ponder on what I'd just heard. I knew it was the Lord; I've heard His still, small voice before, but this was different. I felt as if He was calling me to Him. Calling me to go deeper and find out what He'd just spoken to me. I felt that He wanted me to search the mystery of what He had just said. I ran down-stairs to the basement and started delving into the phrase He spoke to me. I grabbed my cell phone and went to my dictionary app. I chose to research the word "speak" in more detail. I knew what the word meant, but God said that word for a reason. It was that word that opened up who I was and what I was sent in the earth to do. So, I found the word "speak" and found several definitions, but I felt the Lord instructing me to go further. As I looked deeper, I came across this definition that God made me stop on to research: [*To serve as a Spokesperson-found in Merriam-Webster Dictionary © 2016*] I looked up the word "spokesperson" and found the following definition: [*A spokesperson is a man or a woman who speaks for or represents someone or something-found in Merriam-Webster's Dictionary © 2016*].

The word "spokesperson" made me think of the word "representative", so I felt the Lord speak to me to look at the synonyms, and I was obedient. As I looked at the synonyms, I saw these words: [*mouth, mouthpiece, point-man, point-person, PROPHET, speaker, spokesman-found in Merriam-Webster's Dictionary © 2016*].

I immediately threw my cell phone across the room. I was in complete and total shock. With tears in my eyes, I yelled out, "Lord, I'm no prophet! I can't be a prophet; people hate prophets! Please, Lord. I can sing for you; please let me just sing the gospel!" There was a silence for what seemed to go on forever, but it was just a pause in our conversation. He replied to me with a stern, but loving voice, "I didn't call you to sing. You will do what I called you forth to do." After that, He didn't say anything else.

The Lord calling me forth to be His prophet didn't sit well with me. Telling me who I was in Him didn't stop the tears immediately. I was still questioning why I was in

Lexington because I still didn't understand what God was doing. On March 28th 2013, the Lord said to me that I had to die so that Christ could live through me. This helped me to realize that my life wasn't about me, nevertheless, I still fought with my calling.

It wasn't until June of 2013 that I finally gave the Lord a raw and unquestioned "yes". I stopped running, crying, and questioning the Lord, and I finally accepted my true identity. Even today, I still pinch myself because I would have never believed that the Lord would want to use me in such a grandiose way. I wanted to be a nurse with all that was within me, but the Lord had other plans. I remember saying, "Lord, I could have really helped people as a nurse. I could have impacted the world." I could feel His smile, His warmth, and His embrace. The Lord knew that if He would have left me to my own desires, I would have completed nursing school, but I would have never felt complete because my true calling was to advance His kingdom. God is the ultimate employer. I've heard it said that God will give you a job that you're not qualified for. He gave me a position in His kingdom and it came with full benefits and perks that the world cannot match.

The Lord Said:

I will never grow tired of loving you. I never sleep nor do I slumber, for My love is forever. It is unconditional and it is complete. You are not able to fully understand My love for you, but just trust My love and let it purify you; let it set you apart. Let it meet you at the point of your need. My love can find you where you are in your life and spark a consuming fire that will purge you and create in you a clean heart. Let Me do this cleanse in you and make you whole. For I have a mighty work for you to do. I am the only one who knows your heart, and I am the only one who can mend the brokenness of your heart. I am the only one who knows how to handle your heart, so give Me your loss, pain, regret, rejection, depression, anger, trust issues, mistreatments, and all that has embittered you, and I will in turn give you joy, peace, happiness, excitement, loyalty, trust, protection, mercy, grace, and above all else, a love that will never end. Trust Me for your very life. Give Me you and stop running. I will never hurt you; I only want what's best you - my best! I love you.

Precious Thoughts:

- *Be who God created you to be.*
- *Remember that God's calling over your life is far better than what you could ever imagine.*
- *God loves you forever.*
- *Seek God's plan for your life, and chase after it.*
- *Be encouraged.*
- *Know that there is a purpose for your existence.*
- *True identity is hidden in Christ Jesus.*
- *Practice humility.*

Chapter Nine
Many Are Called, Few Are Chosen

"I sent you, first", is what the Lord told me. I'll never forget those words. They became louder and even more prevalent every day since He spoke those words to me. When I first heard Him speak this to me, I thought He meant one thing, and it turned out to be something I could have never imagined. I thought the Lord meant that He sent me first to Lexington on behalf of my family, but the more He revealed to me my destiny, the more I knew it was much bigger than my limited scope. I was despondent, in an unfamiliar place, in a basement, and in darkness.

I was crying when I arose from the basement where I was living, and I went to the front door and looked out at the street. With tears streaming down my cheeks, I opened my mouth and asked the Lord, "Why am I here?" That's when He spoke those words that completely changed my entire focus. What I was doing was focusing on what I was going through and not where I was called to. I was focusing on my circumstances, the pain, the confusion, the isolation, and the breaking. Not one time did I focus on the process, the outcome, or on His promises. I soon found out that it wasn't about me, but about the grand-master plan that I was a part of. The Lord's grandest plan for my life was unfolding as I was living it. Not only had I been called but I was chosen for something greater than myself.

It's Not My Story; It's His Story!

Many things began to happen while I was in the basement. I knew that I was changing and I also knew that I needed guidance. I started searching for a church that could mentor and help me. Even at my lowest point, I wanted God to intervene. I still belonged to Him and I so desperately wanted Him near me. [*Even in distressful and dreadful times, the Lord still guides us. The Lord will use the dark periods in your life to draw you closer to Him. In order to grow, a seed needs darkness for it to breakthrough into the light*].

On New Year's Eve of 2012, I decided to attend a church I heard so much about through a co-worker of mine. I wanted to feel the Lord in my life, and I knew that God had led me to this church. I totally enjoyed the service, and I decided that it was the church for me. I could see myself growing in that church, and I needed to be grounded because I was going through a major shifting in my life. I walked into this church a few months before God called me to be His prophet. The church that I attended back home in Cleveland was a non-denominational church that believed and operated in the five-fold ministry.

Many are Called, Few are Chosen

[*The five-fold ministry offices are gifts that Christ gave for the nurturing and equipping of His church.*] *Ephesians 4:11-12: "And He Himself gave some to be apostles, some prophets, some evangelists, and some pastors, and some teachers, for the equipping of the saints for the work of ministry, for the edifying of the Body of Christ."*

The church I was led to in Lexington was a Baptist church, but it didn't feel Baptist to me. I felt free and I felt like I could be myself there. Early on while attending the church, God called me forth as His prophet, but I kept it very quiet. Not a lot of people knew who I really was. I didn't even know how to be a prophet so I kept my lips close together. For a little over a year, I was quiet about my calling, but eventually, I began to gather with other prophetic and apostolic church members, so I didn't feel alone in my calling. There were others called as well, and God led me straight to them.

I started to really delve into the "church life," wanting to attend church as much as possible because it literally kept me sane. Attending church and surrounding myself with people who could push me towards my destiny was like winning the lottery. During this time, the Lord started to open up to me more and more. I started to hear His still, small voice clearer. I started to pray and seek the Lord more, even though I was still in the basement. As I allowed the church to grow me up spiritually, I began to feel that the church wasn't ready for who I was, plus, I wasn't quite ready to let leadership know my secret either.

So, I began to join different ministries within the church. I joined the creative arts ministry because of writing and poetry. However, the Lord clearly didn't use me in that ministry. The Lord blessed me to sing, so I tried to use my talent in the church's choir. I was planted there for a while, but the Lord shut that down as well because I'm not anointed to minister through song, even though I can sing. The Lord took me out of the music ministry. It seemed as if I never had the time to go to choir rehearsal. It wasn't until I had a prophetic dream that I knew what ministry I was called to. It was in May of 2014 when I had this peculiar dream.

I dreamed that I was at an amusement park with my pastor and his family. In the dream, I was portrayed as one of his children. I was small in stature and walking alongside him. My pastor's wife was in front of us, and she attended to their three children. She kept speaking the same words to me as we all walked from one area of the park to another area. She would tell me, "Now, make sure you listen to everything he's saying, okay?" I would nod my head "yes" and keep walking. My pastor had his arm around me as if he was explaining things to me and I was hanging on to every word he spoke. This was the entire dream. I knew that the Lord was calling me to leadership.

Many are Called, Few are Chosen

[*If you are called to be an Apostle, Prophet,
Evangelist, Pastor, or Teacher, then you are called to be a
front-runner. A Prophet is one of the foundational positions
of the Five Fold Ministry. This order is set by God through
Jesus Christ. Prophets are called to lead*].

I completely ran from the thought of being in
leadership at the church. I thought I didn't have what it took
to lead God's people anywhere. Those thought patterns
were the evidence of my inexperience. God doesn't "call" the
qualified; He qualifies the "called." I was quiet about that
dream for nearly a month, afraid of the rejection I might face.
I wasn't sure if the pastor or leadership of the church would
believe that I was called to lead, but I felt so strongly that I
had to bring it to their attention.

The Sunday that I decided to approach the pastor, I
had some family come down to visit from Cleveland. They
came to church and enjoyed the service, but I let them know
to head back to the house because I needed to stay behind
to speak with the pastor about my dream and what I was
sent to the church to do. I was so nervous that I almost
backed out. Of course, the enemy would have celebrated my
defeat if I had backed away from being obedient to the Lord,
but I foiled his celebration. I actually brought the dream up to
my pastor's wife because I felt more comfortable telling her
about it than my pastor. When I told her my dream, I was
kind of beating around the bush, but she thought I was trying

to ask her if I could be her armor bearer or assistant. I kindly declined that position and explained to her that I was called to leadership, but somehow, it came out that I was called to preach, which isn't what I had in mind. She called the pastor over so that he could hear what I was saying for himself, and I was completely caught off guard. I began to whisper and talk like a little timid child. I eventually got the nerve to tell him that I was called, but for some reason, I didn't say lead; I said to preach because that's what they wanted to hear.

I regret not fully disclosing who I was at that moment. Nevertheless, it wouldn't have mattered because ultimately, it would come out who I was and it didn't turn out in my favor, for the pastor did not incorporate the five-fold ministry. I began to feel pressure from the Lord on what I was really sent to the church to do. The Lord revealed to me that prayer was missing at the church and I felt the Holy Spirit drawing me into a life of prayer, and to introduce it to the church.

I found myself asking the Lord on a nightly basis, what He desired of me. He told me that He wanted me to pray because He hears me. I began to go to the church earlier than normal just to pray over the church. It wasn't too long before I was asked to prepare a fasting and prayer schedule for the upcoming women's conference at the church. This assignment catapulted my desire to introduce prayer to the church. The fasting and prayer schedule that the Lord helped me prepare was very successful, and it helped the women leaders spiritually. The Lord got all the credit, and I was so happy that He used me in such an awesome way, but that feeling was short-lived. The plan to bring a prayer ministry into the church never came into existence. It was rejected by the pastor simply because I didn't compromise. As a prophet of God, I am not to compromise to fit into a man-made mold. I wasn't allowed to introduce the prayer ministry because I admitted to being a prophet. This rejection almost became my undoing.

No one deserves to be rejected, but rejection can save your life. I almost despised my small beginnings, but I praise the Lord because, in the long run, I completed an assignment that only I was chosen to do. Obedience is far better than sacrifice. *I Samuel 15:22: "So Samuel said: 'has the Lord as great delight in burnt offerings and sacrifices, as in obeying the vice of the Lord? Behold, to obey is better than sacrifice, and to heed than the fat of rams.'"*

Personal Prayer:

My Heavenly Father, full of grace and mercy: I want to thank You from the bottom of my heart because You changed me. I am no longer the same person. You took me and completely changed my way of life. I no longer do the things I used to do, I no longer chase after the things that satisfied my flesh, and I no longer have an urge for wicked things. You see, I've been saved since I was 11 years old, and when I gave my life to Jesus and accepted His free gift of salvation, I didn't know that I would be tested, rejected, humiliated, hurt, hated, scorned, used, abused, mistreated, lied on, judged unfairly, beaten, brainwashed, and ultimately left destitute. No one told me that You knew me from the beginning of time and that You never left my side. I had to go through everything I went through to get to You. Everything that was unlike You drove me into Your arms, Lord. All of my hardships broke me, and that was when You whispered to me, "Finally." I was spiritually dead, broken and spinning out of control. I was being pulled into a perpetual downward spiral that ultimately led me to Your feet, and I am forever grateful it did. No longer shall I allow the enemy to live inside of me because I'm more than a conqueror through Christ Jesus. I am who You say that I am, and I stand on Your word and will not be told otherwise. Father, You created me to worship You with my entire existence and to spread the gospel of Jesus Christ. I am a living testimony, and I will tell it wherever I go that Jesus is Lord over my life, and there's nothing anyone can say to me to make me change my mind. I am sold out. To You, Lord, be all the glory, honor, and praise forever. Amen.

Precious Thoughts:

- *Always ask for wisdom and guidance.*
- *Search the true meaning of what you are called to do in the world.*

- *Don't be afraid of stepping into what you are called to be.*
- *Your life will eventually help someone else live.*
- *Make time for the Lord. He desires to pour into you daily.*
- *God loves and rewards your obedience.*
- *Always stay prayerful to the Lord.*

Chapter Ten
The Light Bulb Effect

I'm an insomniac. I've never slept well because I always had so much on my mind. Even as a little girl, I had this issue. It seems as if my brain goes into overdrive when it's time for bed. I believe that I was made just like this on purpose. The Lord likes to speak to me in the wee hours of the morning. My revelatory senses are at a ten in the middle of the night. My prophetic dreams and visions came almost instantaneously when He called me forth as His prophet. The dreams and visions were sent to wake me up and show me who I am.

When I moved out of the basement, God started streaming dreams and visions at me that allowed me to know the level of the prophetic I would be operating in. *Numbers 12:6: "Then He said, 'hear now My words: if there is a prophet among you, I, the Lord, make myself known to him in a vision; I speak to him in a dream.'"*

It's Just a Dream…Or Is It?

I couldn't close my eyes without having some type of vivid dream or unorthodox vision. Even before I was called to be a prophet of the Lord, I would have dreams that I was afraid to tell other people because the dreams or visions were unexplained. I remember when I was a little girl, I would have dreams of outer space, movies and songs that frightened me, tidal waves, and mass destruction. I didn't have these encounters all the time, but when I did, it was hard for me to forget them. The visions and dreams would be so disturbing to me that I would have periods of time that I would be afraid to sleep. I didn't understand why I had dreams like that. I used to think to myself that little girls shouldn't have dreams that were so complicated. I wanted to have dreams of me and "My Little Pony" or "Strawberry Shortcake"; instead, I would have reoccurring nightmares that were way too deep for a five-year old.

Let's rewind to around May of 2012, before I was sent packing southward to Kentucky. I had a dream that I'll never forget. This dream would be the beginning of a stream of prophetic dreams that the Lord was using to awaken my revelatory anointing. [*God created the prophets and the prophetic, because He is prophetic Himself. So, His prophets must in turn become in tune with revelation and revelatory awakening. Revelatory means to make something known, or to reveal something in an unusual way*].

My dream began with me sleeping on a couch in a house I didn't recognize. I was waking up to utter silence. I was stretching and looking around at my surroundings, trying to figure out where everyone was. I was looking for my family. I began to call out to my family, and the only person who was in the dream with me was my younger sister. I got up from the couch and proceeded to walk around, looking for everyone. I asked my sister where our mom was and she told me that she was gone. "Gone? What do you mean she's gone?" In the dream, I was starting to pace back and forth because I couldn't find my mother; it was actually making me nervous.

I began calling for her in the house, yelling for her and waiting for her to answer me back, but I got no response. I began to demand that my sister tell me where our mother was. I was getting frantic by this time. My sister kept telling me that she was gone, but one phrase that she spoke made me stop looking and caused me to ponder. As I continued to grill my sister on the whereabouts of our mother, she began to get agitated as well. She said to me, "She's just gone. I don't know where she went; she just vanished." In the dream, I contemplated what my sister said to me. "Vanished?," I asked. "What do you mean she vanished? How did she just vanish?" She then replied with words that painted a picture in my memory of absolute terror. "I don't know, Eboney. She just vanished. It's like she just disappeared."

At that instant, I knew exactly what had transpired. It was as if my brain made clear to me what had been broadcast to my spirit. It was as if the Lord had given me full awareness of what happened to my mother in an instant. I ran to a big picture window that I saw and flung it open. There were no clouds in the sky. I reached outside of the window and cried aloud, "Jesus, please wait for me. Take me with you!" My mother was caught in the rapture! I began to weep uncontrollably and tears filled my eyes almost to the point where I couldn't see. I screamed for Jesus to take me, and He told me that He couldn't take me with Him. He said I had to stay. I screamed as loud as I could that I didn't want to stay. I demanded that He come back and take me with Him. "It's not time for you to come. You have to stay and I'll come back for you." I said to Jesus that I knew He wasn't coming back again. I knew Him, took Him as my Savior and Lord, and that He had made a mistake. He spoke for the last time to me saying that I had to stay, and then, I heard His voice no more. I was completely devastated.

I wept remorsefully and I fell to my knees sobbing with my face in my hands. I felt like all hope was gone. I felt completely ruined and hopeless. This feeling intensified while I was dreaming. I had no way to escape how I was feeling; it was like my dejection was permanent. Then I heard a voice coming out of the darkness of the house that ignited my emotions. I was overtaken by fear and despair. I couldn't see who was talking to me, but I could feel his words penetrate to the very core of my being. The things he said to me caused me to become frozen. I knew that it was the devil speaking directly to me. He said to me, "Look at you! He came for you, but where were you? You were somewhere sleeping and now you're left alone with me. You're nothing and you're going to die." All I could do was scream, and that's when my mother eventually called me on my cell phone and awakened me from the worst dream I ever had. To me, it was a nightmare.

The Lord didn't reveal the meaning of that dream to me in its entirety until I moved to Kentucky. I was never in the habit of asking what my dreams and visions meant, but I was anxious to know what the Lord was saying to me in that dream. That dream was not only prophetic in its entirety, but it also allowed me to know that I was called to speak the gospel to the nations.

The interpretation of that dream is just as profound as the dream itself. This is what the Lord told me it meant: In the dream, I was asleep, and therefore, I missed the rapture. The Lord said that many of His children will miss this day because of their spiritual slumber. He said to me that His children are asleep spiritually and complacent in their walk with Him, therefore, they will miss their moment of visitation. "Just because you're saved doesn't mean you know Me and serve Me," He said.

Next, in the dream, all was quiet and still. I didn't hear any movement; it was so silent. I had no discernment on what was taking place at the beginning of my dream. Even with the dead silence, I still thought everything was normal. I didn't notice the change until it was too late. The Lord then explained to me the position I played in the dream and also the position my sister played. He explained to me that my sister represented an unbeliever while I was a lukewarm believer. Being an unbeliever was the reason my sister was oblivious to what had happened and she really didn't care to know what happened to our mother.

Lukewarm believers are mentioned in the book of Revelations, chapter 3:15-17: *"I know your works, that you are neither cold nor hot. I could wish you were cold or hot. So then, because you are lukewarm, and neither cold nor hot, I will vomit you out of My mouth. Because you say, 'I am rich, have become wealthy, and have need of nothing,' and do not know that you are wretched, miserable, poor, blind, and naked."* I wasn't vigilant or watchful until the Day of the Lord came. I was sleeping as if I had time or as if I knew I was going to heaven, and that clearly wasn't the case.

Next, I became frantic because I noticed that something wasn't right. I didn't see my mother. This was something normal to me, but sensing that she had been removed induced panic. The Lord told me that the ones who don't know Him fully will be in this state of mind during the day of the Lord, and everyone who thought they were blameless before the Lord will start to panic when the normal is removed. The next revelation of the dream was the Lord giving me full knowledge of what transpired when my sister said that my mother just "vanished" and "disappeared." He allowed me to have full awareness of the fact that Jesus came and that I totally missed the day of the Lord. 1 Thessalonians, chapter 4:16-17 talks about this moment: *"For the Lord Himself will descend from heaven with a shout, with the voice of an archangel, and with the trumpet of God. And the dead in Christ will arise first. Then we who are alive and remain shall be caught up together with them in the clouds to meet the Lord in the air. And thus, we shall always be with the Lord."*

The big picture window signified the entire scope of Jesus. In other words, "the bigger picture," and "the window of opportunity" being missed. There were no clouds in the sky, and the sky was the bluest I had ever seen. The color "blue" in prophetic dreams can represent "heaven" or "heavenly visitation." Clouds can represent chariots or angelic vehicles. Again, 1 Thessalonians, chapter 4:17 talks about the clouds. Now, as I realized what took place, I immediately cried out to Jesus, but it was too late. Jesus saying that I had to stay was my fate for not fully following after Him. The Lord told me that narrow is the gate which leads to everlasting life, and few will find that gate, but wide is the gate and broad is the way that leads to destruction, and that even those who said they would follow Him ended up on the broad path to the wide gate.

The Bible talks of this in Matthew chapter 7 verses 13 and 14: *"Enter by the narrow gate; for wide is the gate and broad is the way that leads to destruction, and there are many who go in by it. Because narrow is the gate and difficult is the way which leads to life, and there are few who find it."* The wrong gate seals their fate and many don't even know it. Many Christians believe that when they were born again that it guaranteed them eternal life with Jesus, but the Lord was clearly showing me that this is not true. Many Christians are not going to be caught up in the sky with Jesus when He comes a second time. Matthew chapter 7 verses 21 through 23 says: *"Not everyone who says to Me, 'Lord, Lord,' shall enter the kingdom of heaven, but he who does the will of My Father in heaven. Many will say to Me in that day, 'Lord, Lord, have we not prophesied in Your name, cast out demons in Your name, and done many wonders in Your name?' And then I will declare to them, 'I never knew you; depart from Me, you who practice lawlessness.'*

God also says that people who fulfill the lust of the flesh will not enter into the kingdom of God. Galatians chapter 5 verses 16 through 21 says: *"I say then; 'Walk in the Spirit, and you shall not fulfill the lust of the flesh. For the flesh lusts against the Spirit, and the Spirit against the flesh; and these are contrary to one another, so that you do not do the things that you wish. But if you are led by the Spirit, you are not under the law. Now the works of the flesh are evident, which are: adultery, fornication, uncleanness, lewdness, idolatry, sorcery, hatred, contentions, jealousies, outbursts of wrath, selfish ambitions, dissensions, heresies,*

*envy, murders, drunkenness, revelries, and the like; of which
I tell you beforehand just as I also told you in time past, that
those who practice such things will not inherit the kingdom of
God.'"*

As I begged and pleaded, I could not get Jesus to
come back for me; nothing I said changed His mind. I would
have to suffer in the world without Him. He removed His spirit from the earth and I fell into total despair. The Lord allowed
me to know what it will feel like when the Holy Spirit is with-
drawn from the earth. The Holy Spirit testifies of Jesus, so
when Jesus left me and stopped speaking with me, I felt the
Holy Spirit no more. The Holy Spirit is the hope of the world,
and when He was removed, so was my hope.

My emotions were heightened during this part of the
dream. The Lord allowed me to understand fully what despair was. This feeling that I had was beyond fear; this was
complete hopelessness that I would never see Jesus again.
[Fear means to be afraid of something or someone or to
have an unpleasant emotion caused by being aware of some
type of danger-found in Merriam-Webster's Dictionary ©
2016]. Despair is altogether different. [To despair means to
no longer have any hope or belief that a situation will im-
prove or change-found in Merriam Webster's Dictionary ©
2016]. I was allowed to be cognizant of the feeling those who
are left behind will feel once they realize that the hope of the
world is absent from creation and this feeling was in-
escapable.

The Light Bulb Effect

The Lord then began to reveal what the darkness meant in the dream; this was the most frightening part of the entire dream. Darkness can represent death, sorrow, distress, destruction, and judgment. The voice I heard was coming from a place of darkness. What the voice was saying to me were all the things that the devil tells God's creation daily. But in the dream, there was no hope, therefore, what he was saying felt true. The devil said that I was "nothing" so the Lord explained to me that with Christ, we are something; without Him, we are nothing.

This was the revelation of the dream that the Lord sent to me. It's still vivid in my memory, and He charged me to tell others what I had seen. I asked Him when I would be given the opportunity to tell people what I had been shown. I told Him that I didn't know how to reach the masses. The Lord was quiet with giving me instructions on how to tell others about my dream until now, so this is the "light bulb effect"....in the literal sense. This book is allowing His words to be made manifest through my testimony. His purpose for who I am is being made manifest as well.

This one dream solidified my purpose here on earth... a purpose I've had long before I even knew I was a prophet to God's people. God knew beforehand that this dream was to be told to the entire world. He knew that I would not botch this assignment once given the opportunity to be obedient to Him. He didn't need to tell me when to release the dream to the world. My "yes" to Him made the alignment assured. My "yes" made room for me and my assignment. I've had plenty more dreams and visions. I've released the ones the Lord has permitted me to release, and I've remained silent about the ones He has not given me the unction to release.

So, I have been given a great assignment that the Lord will see to completion. I have the honor of speaking to His people and to bring restoration to His church. I am sent to turn the hearts of the people of God back toward Him. This one prophetic dream summed up what I will continue to do until I've completed my assignment. I thank the Lord for His will over my own will. His will has so much more meaning and joy than my own. It's no easy task, but it's worth it.

The Lord Said:
"I am building you up. I am perfecting my workmanship in you. Do not resist the process. This is all a part of the process; do not resist My hand. I will prove you before many. This is my way and it will prevail. No one will resist, but my remnant will be proven before many. The day of the Lord will proceed with My remnant being perfected to do the supernatural after."

Precious Thoughts:

- *Don't resist the plans the Lord has for you.*

The Light Bulb Effect

- *Don't be afraid to walk in your destiny.*
- *You are meant for greatness, so start shining.*
- *The Lord knows what He is doing in your life; after all, He created you.*

Chapter Eleven
The Weeping Prophet

Jeremiah was called the "weeping prophet" in the Old Testament. It's actually kind of endearing that this chapter is called, "The Weeping Prophet." At first, I really didn't identify with this particular prophet, but as God was dealing with me and kept me in isolation, I found myself weeping and being somber most of the time. God deals with me in this manner. He took things from me that I thought I needed to survive. He took me from my immediate family in Cleveland, He took my nursing education from me, He took away my money and He took away my jobs as well. He took away everything that kept me from submitting to Him. I was bare and naked before Him to the point where I had no other choice but to give in to His will. That's exactly how He wanted me...destitute and alone. That may seem somewhat harsh, but that's the only way for me to explain my isolation. Alone, naked, emptied...a ready vessel for the Potter to reform.

Jeremiah 18:1-6: "The word which came to Jeremiah from the Lord, saying: 'Arise and go down to the potter's house, and there I will cause you to hear My words.' Then I went down to the potter's house, and there he was making something at the wheel. And the vessel that he made of clay was marred in the hand of the potter; so he made it again into another vessel, as it seemed good to the potter to make. Then the word of the Lord came to me saying: 'O house of Israel, can I not do with you as this potter?' says the Lord. 'Look, as the clay is in the potter's hand, so are you in My hand, O house of Israel.'"

As I stated earlier, preparation comes before purpose, and transformation comes before duty. I came to the realization that God was going to perfect me as His prophet one way or another; it would all depend on my cooperation. The Lord disciplines His children for their good because it produces a righteousness in them that He approves.

Discipline isn't something that we want to endure, but in the long run, it's needed to grow in every area of our lives. Hebrews 12:7-12: *"If you endure chastening, God deals with you as sons; for what son is there whom a father does not chasten? But if you are without chastening, of which all have become partakers, then you are illegitimate and not sons. Furthermore, we have had human fathers who corrected us, and we paid them respect. Shall we not much more readily be in subjection to the Father of spirits and live? For they indeed for a few days chastened us as seemed best to them, but He for our profit, that we may be partakers of His holiness. Now no chastening seems to be joyful for the present, but painful; nevertheless, afterwards it yields the peaceable fruit of righteousness to those who have been trained by it."* I thank the Lord for the discipline He provided. It showed me that He desired to perfect me so that I would honor Him with my life and obedience.

The Rejection Files Pt.2

I can remember the dream where I was walking with my former pastor and his family; it felt so right to be a part of his family. I knew that being a part of their family meant that I was appointed to that particular church body. I was on assignment by God for the church. I wish I could say that I'm still attending that church, but I'm no longer there.

As I began to accept the responsibility as a leader at the church, the Lord began to speak His desire to me and told me the direction He wanted the church to go in. I tried to keep a low profile in the leadership ministry because only a few people knew I was a prophet. [*One of the many exploits of a prophet is to bring direction and guidance to the people of God*]. I had an innate desire to want to see this church flourish because it wasn't flowing the way the Lord intended, and He had so much He wanted to do through this church. [*Prophets are sent ones, and they sense when the move of God is needed. It will grieve a prophet when the authenticity of God is absent*].

The more I attended the church, the more I felt that something was truly missing. I connected my faith with what the Word of God said; that prayer is the most essential thing. *Acts 6:1-4: 'Now in those days, when the number of the disciples was multiplying, there arose a complaint against the Hebrews by the Hellenists, because their widows were ne-*

glected in the daily distribution. Then the twelve summoned the multitude of the disciples and said, 'It is not desirable that we should leave the Word of God and serve tables. Therefore, brethren, seek out from among you seven men of good reputation, full of the Holy Spirit and wisdom, whom we may appoint over this business; but we will give ourselves continually to prayer and to the ministry of the Word.'"

I was sent to bring prayer into a prayerless church. Everything was moving in the church except prayer. It's not uncommon for churches now to remove practices from the church that were done in the beginning. I prayed to the Lord for my mandate to be made manifest so that I could be obedient. He did just that when the church was preparing for their annual Women's Conference in October 2014. I volunteered to create a prayer and fasting schedule for the conference. It was a success, and soon after that, the Lord gave me a blueprint for an intercessory prayer ministry at the church.

I was told that there was some sort of prayer at the church at one point in time, but it dwindled and became non-existent. I knew that there were individuals praying and that they had an inconsistent prayer line, but it wasn't what God was calling for. The Lord wanted a ministry dedicated to prayer for this church and He wanted me to start it. My prayer life, at that time, was thriving. It began in the basement where the Lord started teaching me how to pray for my family first. He was teaching me how to intercede, travail, and war in prayer for my family. It was a long process, but it was extremely effective. I had prayed inconsistently prior to moving to Lexington, and most of the time, I'd only prayed when my life was in shambles, never understanding that prayer should have been the central tactic instead of the last resort.

I was totally obedient to the assignment given to me by the Lord. I knew full well what I was to do, but I was fearful. I hadn't seen any prophets walking around at the church, but I knew some were there because God showed me the prophets and prophetic people at the church, and I quickly became close friends with them. When I found out that there were other prophets at the church, I felt more eager to present what God had given me to share with the church, but the roadblock I had to get past was the pastor.

When I began to release what the Lord wanted to see happen for the church, the pastor didn't seem too interested. I wrote a 13-page document explaining why prayer was so important, and he didn't read it for almost a month because he said it was "too long." After some pushing by his wife, he finally read the document, commended it, and then said that he was looking forward to seeing what God was going to do with the ministry. The Holy Spirit had written the requirements for the ministry (through me) in a few hours and I was completely amazed. I couldn't have done that by myself. After they were presented, I then created a 22 slide Power-

Point presentation. It felt good to see what the Lord was getting ready to do.

By this time, I was getting trained in the prophetic and felt confident with what the Lord was teaching me about prayer. Now, in the presentations that I presented to the pastor, I did indicate that prophets and intercessors would need to teach all the material, and at first glance, the pastor was on board. It wasn't until I had offended his wife shortly after the presentation at the women's bible study that things took a change for the worst. I corrected the pastor's wife during a bible study discussion, and instead of asking me to stay behind after bible study so we could talk about it, she told the pastor to correct me. I had been rejected so many times in my life prior to this incident, but this was completely different coming from the church's pastor. It was more painful and it took longer for me to heal. What the pastor did was almost blasphemous because of the things he said, not only to me but to another dear friend of mine who is also a prophet. *[Blasphemous means to treat a holy place or object with great disrespect]*.

I Peter 1:15-16: "But as He who called you is holy, you also be holy in all your conduct, because it is written, 'Be holy, for I am holy.'" Since my friend and I are vessels of God, to speak what the pastor said to us was extremely profane to God Himself, not to us personally. Here are a few things that the pastor said about me:

- I was called confused. I was told to be quiet.
- I was told that prophets were not accepted at the church.
- I was told that I was not allowed to prophesy or pray for anyone at the church in fear of them wanting to follow me.
- I was told that the five-fold ministry wasn't taught or preached at the church, and if I was a "so-called" prophet, I should leave and find a church that had prophets.
- I was told that I was out of order for seeking training in the prophetic.
- I was told that I was operating under familiar spirits, which was borderline "witchcraft."

Those were only some of the things the pastor said to the two of us. We were both devastated and totally crushed by what he said. After the detachment from reality, he then hugged us and said that he did what he did in "love." I felt the rejection in my core. The Holy Spirit allowed me to know that He was grieved, and I wasn't able to focus on ministry at the church anymore. *Ephesians 4:29-30: "Let no corrupt word proceed out of your mouth, but what is good for necessary edification, that it may impart grace to the hearers. And do not grieve the Holy Spirit of God, by whom you were sealed for the day of redemption."*

Soon after that meeting, the pastor started preaching erroneous sermons. He was attacking prophets and speaking error over the people of God because of his dislike for me. The meeting happened in January of 2015, and the Lord told me that my assignment was over and I stepped down and departed ways with the church in February of 2015. In that small time-frame, I tried to get back on track, but knowing that the pastor didn't respect who I was and what I was sent to do made it unbearable. I was unable to sit in a church where the pastor wasn't speaking to me. He would turn his back on me and continued to speak ill of me from the pulpit.

While in that small time-frame, the pastor gave all who were in the leadership ministry an assignment to complete. He gave us a small window to complete it in and I was extremely hesitant because of what had transpired prior to this assignment. I literally had to pray and ask the Holy Spirit to complete the assignment for me because I didn't want to disrespect the pastor. The name of the assignment was, "accountability." He asked each leader three questions which were: What were the three ministry goals we would like to accomplish, what area of ministry did we feel we could assist in leadership at the church, and what did we need from him.

This is what I wrote in the assignment given to me: *"The foremost goal that I wanted to accomplish here at TG was the Intercessory Prayer Ministry. I totally believe that God called me to begin "real" prayer in His sanctuary at TG.*

The second goal I would like to accomplish is to become an effective leader here at TG. I answered the call to lead, not necessarily preach. Not all prophets are called to preach. I have been called to be a "Watchman" and to be a part of something great that is orchestrated and set up by the Holy Spirit.

Here at TG, there seems to be a lack of cohesiveness and unity among the leadership, and after doing some observing and discerning, it seems that all the ministers in training are being trained to "preach" instead of being mentored to "lead." I fully understand that ministers will be called upon to preach the gospel and that we all need to be ready to answer that call, but I can honestly say that I have not been mentored in that area since I announced that I am a leader. I do not see how I will be ready to "preach" my initial sermon within six months when I, for instance, have never been sat down and asked anything about myself, where I came from, why I joined TG, why I feel that I'm called to service, and what I'm called to do for the Kingdom. No one ever asked me about me, and that's important because everyone isn't called to "preach" or be a shepherd.

When I approached the first lady and yourself (Pastor) with the news that I was called, I remember you smiled at me and said, "Okay good, we will get you prepared to preach your initial sermon in about six months from now." I thought to myself, "preach?" I don't know one thing about preaching, let alone how to write a sermon. I honestly believed that leadership at TG was to mentor its leaders in the art of leading. Learning how to co-exist with other leaders, other ministries within the body of Christ, to help lead and properly care for God's flock, and to lead outside the four walls of the church in the area we've been called to.

Since there is no core foundation of prayer here at TG, my other ministry goal here may not see the light. I wanted to teach and prepare God's intercessors on the fundamentals of intercessory prayer. The intercessory prayer ministry was something the Holy Spirit wanted to use at TG to bring in a new focus and discipline that is clearly not being enforced. TG is not a praying church, and therefore, the flock has no covering, power or presence. The outline of the ministry was not of my doing, but of the Holy Spirit. I am but a mere vessel in total submission to His order and mandate. The teaching module was strategically written and formed to allow prayer to be utilized to its fullest capacity. I totally understand that you have a bigger responsibility to cover God's flock and I had hoped to be of some assistance to the shepherd of TG, not a hindrance as I may seem through your perception.

What area of ministry do I feel I could assist in leadership with and why?: The area of ministry I had hoped to be a part of here was intercessory prayer. I do apologize for the repetitiveness of intercessory prayer, but I am called to intercede; that's one of the many mantles of a prophet. I do recall you asking me, when we had our discussion a few Saturdays ago, if I really believed that I held the office of a prophet, and you said that you felt I was confused. I can say to you that I'm not confused at all. I am currently in training and being mentored in the area of the prophetic.

I also recall you saying that day that you do not teach on the five-fold ministry, therefore, you do not preach it, "We don't do that here," assuming "that" meant five-fold ministry, and "here" meaning TG. I can fully respect you, pastor, for your views and ideology. I do not, however, agree with the five-fold ministry not being fully used at TG. I will never disrespect you in any way because you are my shepherd and God placed you over His people at TG, but I do have my own mind and my allegiance is to the divine order of God's kingdom, His Will for my life, and who He called me to be, no matter what anyone else says or believes about me.

I say this because I believed that my leadership role would have been to help TG stay separated from the world. We are all called, but few are chosen to push the kingdom of God further on behalf of Christ Jesus. I completely believe I'm a chosen vessel; I'm called to be holy, I am different, and I see things differently than others. I am very spiritual and I do know God's voice in my life. That's why I know I'm a chosen vessel. If I had the chance to explain my story, I would have revealed more of my plight to you.

The Weeping Prophet

What do I need from you, pastor? What I need from you, pastor, is an understanding that we are all different, and we all bring something great to the body of Christ; that we, as leaders, all have different and special gifts handed down to us from God. There has been tension between us because of what happened during the discussion a few Saturdays ago. I felt like I was blind-sided, belittled, defamed and made to feel inferior during that meeting. It was like you were unleashed upon me, and I can tell you that the offense hit the Holy Spirit that dwells inside of me more than anything else.

I have never felt like such a despondent and dejected person in this manner ever in my life, and it came at the hands of my pastor. Please don't ever do anyone else like that again. Please don't make another one of God's sheep that you have jurisdiction over feel like I did that day. I smiled while I was still at church so that I would not cause a scene, but on the inside, I was completely downtrodden. I felt useless. The things you said to me pierced my heart and I wanted to run, but God commanded me to stay. Being dejected by your pastor would make anyone want to run, leave the church, and question their own identity, but I love you, your family, and God's people too much to leave because of an offense.

The enemy would have loved it if I would have packed up and left TG, but I give no place to the enemy in my life. God is in full control, and my time here is not up. So, upon saying that, if you feel that I would not fit the mold of a leader here, by all means exercise your right as pastor and remove me. I would have no regrets. No matter what you decide, I will completely honor your decision. Thank you for your time and allowing me to answer these questions."

The Lord answered my prayer because He knew that I was not going to be that eloquent, but rather, worldly because of the rejection and bitterness that was creeping in. When I finally left, it was under the direction of the Lord. I didn't hesitate because of the time that I invested in the church. I didn't think twice because the Lord spoke to me and stated that he (the pastor) was not going to stop attacking me until I left. I wrote an exit letter that explained why I was stepping down and leaving the church.

This entire incident catapulted me into a pruning period in my life. God was getting me ready for greater. I didn't so much as cry about what happened to me in this particular church; I was more embittered. I was more concerned about the rejection of prayer and God's hand moving in the church. Prayer wasn't wanted there and it hurt me to see that, but what the Lord was showing me was that when I'm rejected, hated, and persecuted, then it's really Jesus being rejected, hated, and persecuted. I know that I left an impact on that church. Many people contacted me letting me know that I was missed, but the Lord explained to me that I had to leave and that He had greater for me to do.

The next morning after I left the church, I sent my letter to the pastor and his wife, and the Lord laid me down and sent me a prophetic dream to let me know that my assignment was over at TG. In the dream, I was at a funeral procession at a church. I was sitting and talking with a member of the church I had just let. A lot of people were standing and walking while we were still sitting and talking.

As the church was emptying out, I got up and walked out with the member I was talking with on the inside. I then walked up to the hearse and the window came down. A man inside the hearse started speaking to me in Spanish, asking me if I had some change I could give him. I was able to understand every word he spoke to me. He had a dollar and wanted coins in return. So I said to him that I could help him, and as I reached for my purse, I realized that I had left it back at the church. He continued to ask me for help and I said to him, "I left everything back at the church. All that I need to help you with is still in the church."

I was getting ready to go back to the church to get the things that I left, but the back of the hearse began to lift up. I walked slowly to it and saw a woman and three small animals. She was also speaking Spanish, and I asked her if I could help her. She was preparing a place in the back of the hearse for her and the small animals to sleep. She had blankets and she was putting them on the animals and herself. She spoke to me in Spanish that she didn't need any help. I kept asking her to let me help and she repeatedly told me "no." Suddenly, the backdoor of the hearse closed shut. I then began to run back to the church to grab my things that I left, but the doors of the church were closing. I yelled for my friend to hold the doors open, but she couldn't, and I got to the doors too late. I wasn't able to get back in the church.

The Lord revealed the meaning of that dream to me. He was showing me that my time was up at that church and I'd left behind some things that the church needed to use in order to grow. He also showed me that my help was needed but rejected. Lastly, once I exited the church, I wasn't permitted back because I had completed my assignment.

I contemplated whether I should've spoken about this time in my life in this book, and the Lord explained to me that since this is my testimony, I had every right to. There are other people who have been rejected in this manner and the Lord needs you to know that you are not alone. He knows how you feel; He understands what you're going through. You'll make it through. Trust in the Lord because He knows that this will pass and you'll be better and stronger for the next assignment. Understand that what doesn't kill you will indeed make you stronger.

If the Lord appointed you to do something for Him, trust that He will give you the grace to be obedient and to complete it. This test came to not only strengthen my walk with the Lord, but to put His stamp of approval on me yet again. If man rejects me, that doesn't mean that God has rejected me. In fact, it shows that I am following Jesus's footsteps. Remember that He was rejected, hated, and persecuted, and now, He sits at the right-hand of the Lord. We fall to rise again, and a just man falls but a few times, yet, he gets back up with a "right" mind. *Proverbs 24:16: "For a righteous man may fall seven times and rise again, but the wicked shall fall by calamity."*

Prophetic Prayer:

I have a prophetic prayer for someone who may have been told that you are not who God said you are. The enemy is A LIAR! God never lies, and God still speaks even now to His people. I decree and declare that you will walk tall, Apostle, Prophet, Evangelist, Pastor, Teacher, and every man or woman of God. Don't let the labels fool you because God isn't moved by labels, but He is moved by your obedience and trust in Him. You are who He says you are. I declare when He calls you, no one can thwart that calling. You will walk in His power, authority, anointing, and mandate. Go forth with a shout and defiance against the enemy like never before. This is not the time to operate in your flesh but walk in the spirit at ALL times that you may know the perfect will of God. I love you all and stay encouraged and unmovable. Amen.

Precious Thoughts:

- *As you grow in godliness and holiness, stay humble and praise God always.*
- *Loyalty to the Lord will gain you honor in His sight.*
- *Man can persecute you, but remember that the Lord is your shield. No one can harm you when you're doing the will of the Lord.*
- *The Lord will eventually silence the enemy on your behalf; let Him fight for you.*
- *Love your enemies, in spite of their ill feelings toward you.*
- *Truly forgive and move on.*

Chapter Twelve
A Bright Future Ahead

I just want to reiterate something, and that's the fact that I didn't ask for all of this. I didn't ask for the call on my life. I figured that I would become a nurse, make lots of money, marry the guy of my dreams, raise my children, and then, die old and full. Never would I have imagined that God had a completely different plan for my life. The plan I had for my life never mirrored what God had already pre-ordained for me. When I look back over my life, not one time did I ever come to ruin in His eyes. I would eventually know who I was to become, and I am forever indebted to Him and forever grateful that my plans were divinely interrupted. Just like no one ever told me that I had to die, no one ever told me that I could live for Him. I now live unapologetic, unrestricted, full of promise, full of His grace and mercy, being adopted, having dominion, all the while, advancing the kingdom.

The First Shall Be Last, The Last Shall Be First

I love Matthew 20:16. Jesus is speaking a parable of the workers in the vineyard. Even though there is a reward for serving, we should never look for the reward, but serve out of love. *Matthew 20:16: "So the last shall be first, and the first shall be last. For many are called, but few are chosen."*

I often ponder on this scripture because I never placed myself first in anything. I would never see myself in front, leading, a forerunner or in the forefront. How could I leave a legacy for my son or the generations to come after me with that type of mindset?

That's just the thing. My mindset had to change and continue changing in order for me to realize the greatness inside of me. The Lord spoke a word to me while in my storm. He said, *"I am great, so I want to abide in you so that My greatness is shown through you. I will get glory, and you will reap the benefit for being obedient."* God wants His greatness to be shown through His called vessels; I'm a harbinger of His glory. My willingness paved the way for God's greatness to be shown through me. I have a responsibility to uphold. I have the greatest honor of being God's called prophet and paving the way for others to follow.

The legacy the Lord is allowing me to create for the vessels who are following in my footsteps is going to be built on integrity. A monetary legacy is amazing in its own right, but integrity, character, and a hunger for righteousness is what I desire for my son and the next generation. I can remember a prophetic vision that the Lord sent to me while I was still in the basement. It was amazing because He was showing me what I would be doing in the future. In the vision, I saw myself walking on a preset path. I was walking very steadily and circumspectly. I had a look of precision on my face and my hands were outstretched before me. As the vision started to expand, I could see that I was making prominent footprints on the path, and I saw what looked like children following in my footprints. My footprints were so big that the children were taking giant steps into the prints.

I almost forgot about that vision, but God brought it back to my remembrance for such a time as this. The Lord is raising up a remnant who will hearken to His voice and awaken to what they're called in the earth to do. Everything we as people of God will go through in this lifetime will bring us to a point in our lives where the greatness of God will burst forth through us. As we look at ourselves, we should see the workmanship of a fearfully and wonderfully designed creature, and nothing should stop us from believing that we have been sent with a complete purpose. *Psalm 139:14: "I will praise You, for I am fearfully and wonderfully made; marvelous are Your works, and that my soul knows very well."*

Our futures are as bright as our hope in Christ Jesus, for He is our hope and the light of the world. I am still looking towards my bright future. I know full well that instead of dying full like I wanted to before I knew my identity, I will die emptied out. I will have done the will of the Lord, and when I have accomplished all that He has set before me, He will call me home, emptied out and the anointing that I held will be dispersed for the next line of called vessels......FOR HIS GLORY!

A Bright Future Ahead

Personal Prayer:

Father in heaven, I pray to You for Your divine purpose to manifest. Let Your will flourish in the lives of Your people. I pray, Lord, that Your will may come forth so that You may be glorified forever. I long to be obedient to You, Lord. I long to worship You with my obedience. I crave to be near You and feel Your presence. Bless Your people, O Lord, so that we may praise You. Let Your will manifest in our lives so that we may cling to Your Word and promises. Give us a word from You and let us see Your word come forth. Show us Your love and strength; guide and lead us by the hand into Your promises. Please, O Lord, continue to love and keep us safe from all harm. Thank You for our lives, and thank You for giving us back our lives. We love You, Lord. Amen.

Precious Thoughts:

- *Bless the Lord at all times.*
- *He has you in the palm of His mighty hand.*
- *Know that your beginning is not your end.*
- *Let the Lord awaken His greatness inside of you.*
- *Do not apologize for who you are in Christ Jesus.*
- *Never ask how something will happen. Just trust God for the provision needed to move forward to make it happen.*

- *Know that God always has, and always will love you unconditionally.*

Prayer and Affirmations

I want to thank everyone who took the time to read my memoirs. I pray that this book will change a life. I want to make sure that every eye that reads this book understands that Jesus died for them that they may live in the fullness of His glory. Just in case someone may question their salvation, please say this prayer with me:

Dear Lord,

I'm coming to You bare and unashamed to say that I need You in my life. I am tired of living in fear and wondering if I will be with You at the end of all things. I'm tired of the devil running and ruining my life. I don't want him to have control of my life anymore. I know that I've sinned against You, Lord, and I ask right now, for Your forgiveness. I repent for my sins, and I understand that Jesus died in my place on the cross for my sins. I understand that Jesus died for me, rose again, and will return someday for me. Jesus, I accept the gift of salvation. Change me; please be my Savior now. I desire for You to be in control of my life, instead of the devil. Thank You, Jesus, for saving me, and now, I can live for You. I love You, Lord. In Jesus name, I pray. Amen.

I know that may have been a little different for some people reading, but I felt the need to do this. Someone may need that prayer. Also, please read all the prayers in this book and place yourself in each prayer. I also want to help someone change their perception of themselves. Sometimes, we can get caught up in the wrong thoughts and views about ourselves and begin speaking wrong thoughts over our lives. Let's start seeing ourselves how God sees us. Let's start each day off with some confirming affirmations. Here are some affirmations that I speak over myself daily:

- *I am free.*
- *I am saved.*
- *I am needed.*
- *I am successful.*
- *I am a winner.*
- *I am loved.*
- *I will never doubt God.*
- *I am bold in my belief in the Lord Jesus Christ.*
- *I am a complete blessing.*
- *I am truly humbled.*
- *I am always growing.*
- *I am fully prosperous.*
- *I am not poor.*
- *I am the head and not the tail.*
- *I am above and never beneath.*
- *I will lend to many nations and never borrow.*
- *I am a born leader.*
- *I truly stand for the Lord Jesus Christ.*
- *I am a trend-setter.*
- *I speak life, health and prosperity over myself and others.*
- *I am wealthy.*
- *I am a successful business woman/man.*
- *I am a cheerful giver.*
- *I am deadly to the enemy.*

- *I am totally focused.*
- *I am fully forgiven.*
- *I am redeemed.*
- *I am trustworthy.*
- *I am not created for nonsense.*
- *I am walking in my destiny.*
- *I am free from debt.*
- *I am never a loser.*
- *I am healthy.*
- *I am a loyal friend.*
- *I am a prayer warrior.*
- *I am a teacher.*
- *I am a lover of the Lord, Jesus Christ.*
- *I am involved in God's Kingdom.*
- *I am CHOSEN.*
- *I am in tune with the Holy Spirit.*
- *I am fully anointed.*
- *I am able to lay hands and release the anointing.*
- *I do not operate within the confines of this world.*
- *I am Kingdom-minded.*
- *I have the mind of the Lord, Jesus Christ.*
- *I desire to be holy.*
- *I am mindful of my thoughts and speech.*
- *I am a believer in the Lord, Jesus Christ.*
- *I am a true servant of the Lord, Jesus Christ.*
- *I am a responsible leader in my home, ministry, church and work.*
- *I am a great employee.*
- *I am a child of the Most High God.*
- *I am prosperous in everything I do.*

- *I am obedient to God.*
- *I will not lean on my own understanding.*
- *I am a woman/man of purpose.*
- *I am a true wife/husband to my spouse.*
- *I am not foolish or silly.*
- *I will not desire to live in drama.*
- *I am who God says I am.*
- *I will pray for my family and will intercede on their behalf.*
- *I will go in the ways of the Lord, Jesus Christ all the days of my life.*
- *I will lead others to the Lord, Jesus Christ and on correct paths.*
- *I am fully used by God.*
- *I will follow the voice of the Lord.*
- *I am appreciated and faithful in all I do.*
- *I am dedicated to the Kingdom of God.*

believe that these affirmations can change someone's view of themselves. Speaking life over yourself, your situations, your family and your enemies can cause positive reactions instead of negative reactions. The Bible states that death and life lie within the tongue; we can curse or bless with it. *Proverbs 18:21: "Death and life are in the power of the tongue, and those who love it will eat of its fruit."*

I want to leave you all with a prayer that I wrote in the midst of trials and tribulation. Even in the wildernesses of my life, there was light at the end of the tunnel. I knew deep down in my heart that the Lord was in the midst and I desired Him more than anything. I love you all and I pray that God truly is your ALL IN ALL.

Lord, during this test, I want to hear from You. I want to feel You and I want to feel Your presence. I need to know You deeply; I need to hear from You. Please touch me in my intimate place; I want to know You closely. A special closeness is what I desire. Sometimes, I wonder if I please You, Lord. Please keep me because I desire to be pleasing in Your sight. I completely value what You have instilled in me, Lord. You are what I desire.

Since You have called me to this life of servitude, I know that You will provide the power for me to be a blessing to others. You called me righteous. You changed my very nature and I'll forever be grateful to You. I love You with a love that I don't completely understand, but I trust that love and I trust You and Your will for my life. I desire to have a more intimate experience with You, Lord. I want the world to know Jesus through my life. I'll never be the same…I'm not the same as I pray this prayer. I'm sold out. I can no longer be who I used to be; I don't know how to be that person any-more. She is dead and no longer in existence….she was a counterfeit.

Lord, You are more than what I thought I could attain in this life. You have given me a sense of belonging and I want to be more like You every day. Please continue to shape and mold me into the warrior You have destined me to be. I want to be Your voice in this world. I want to be Your feet in this world and I want to worship You with my very existence. Please continue to endow me with Your glory. Lord, continue to allow me to come before You humbly on behalf of Your people and the lost souls. Feel me Lord…search my heart, Lord…feel my love for You. It's genuine; it's true and it's real. This is more than I could possibly imagine.

Please take me higher in You, Lord. Please satisfy my spirit with Your love, grace, mercy, peace, joy, righteousness, justice, and faithfulness. Empty me of myself, and replace me with all of You. I need Thee; I crave Thee, and I desire Thee more than life itself. Take me, capture me, and release me into Your presence for I desire to be in chains for You. Imprison my soul, Lord. Take me and complete me. Never in my wildest dreams have I thought I would desire You more than anything or anyone. For You alone are my love, my knight in shining armor; You are my everlasting sky. You are my morning glory, You are my shimmering night sky, and You are my everything! I need You forever. I take You into my heart and hold You very close to me. Please continue to search me, Lord, and find the damaged parts. Soothe them, mend them and hold me close to You so evil will never bind me again. As long as I have breath in my body, I will live for You forever my King…I love You!

www.ingramcontent.com/pod-product-compliance
Lightning Source LLC
Chambersburg PA
CBHW060939040426
42445CB00011B/932